Terry McCarthy

A Short History of the British Labour Movement

From a Socialist Perspective

Foreword by Dr. Louise Raw

Editor: Sam Clifton-Sprigg

LHMP. TU

ISBN 978-0-9556923-4-5

This book is dedicated to Bill Benfield, former editor of the Morning Star, a lifelong socialist and true friend through good times and bad.

Contents

Foreword by Dr. Louise Raw

The upper echelons of British society have always excelled at preserving and privileging their history.

Kings, Queens, aristocrats and battles are endlessly represented in painting, public and private statuary, book and film. Mainstream historical programming throngs with them, too - I can't be the only Briton who grew up knowing almost as much about Henry VIII's personal life as those of my own family.

When it comes to the history of the working classes, things are different. Very little is included in the school curriculum, and courses have been severely cut at further education level.

Those of us who write and work in the field are used to being told our work is 'niche'. That is, on the face of it, an astonishing assumption: the history and experiences of the vast majority of humanity cannot be 'niche', and more than the 1% can, by very definition, be other than the minority.

There is, in fact, a tremendous, largely unsatisfied thirst for stories of 'real people'. Readers and audiences are not just interested in, but inspired by, the lives and achievements of people who are relatable, and were- or could have been- their own ancestors.

It's of more than superficial importance that these stories be included in the reproduction of knowledge. It's been famously said that 'If you can't see it, you can't be it'- hearing about the great deeds done by 'ordinary' people show us what is possible.

Psychologists too have proved this: in experiments, girls told stories of women's achievements got a measurable boost to their self-esteem.

It is vital that all who are pushed to the margins, whether because of sex, sexuality, race or class, are able to see their culture holding up the mirror to their own lives and experiences.

Our need to know and to tell our human story seems to be an intrinsic part of our nature: cutting us off from them is a deprivation and, in its way, oppression.

For all of these reasons, there has long been a need for a new, readable and truly comprehensive history of the British trade union and labour movement. How and when did the majority, who had the numbers but not the power or wealth, begin to organise and band together? What were the milestones and pitfalls along the way, and how has that past lead us to where we are today?

Filling that gap is a huge undertaking, but 40 years of teaching labour history, combined with 15 years as the director of the National Museum of Labour History, fitted Terry McCarthy well for it.

McCarthy has met many major players in the movement, and has a good memory for anecdote. His research has been thorough, and he combines the scholarly with new and memorable personal details from his own research, like the pearl handled pistol union leader Ben Tillet gave to his daughter Jennie, to protect herself when working for the Dockers' union.

The historical sweep of this book is impressive – discussing industrial relations legislation, McCarthy is able to go back as far as 1349; he extends forward to the rise and leadership of Jeremy Corbyn, and the concomitant 'renaissance in activism'.

The book does not shy away from the disputes within the movement, but provides a realistic account. Nor, thankfully and, sadly, still quite unusually, does McCarthy neglect the importance of women in the movement, from the Bow Matchwomen's strike of 1888 to the wonderful Jayaben Desai at Grunwick.

McCarthy's knowledge and political perspective make this a unique and indispensable guide.

Dr. Louise Raw

March 2017

Author's Preface

Since the election of Jeremy Corbyn as Labour Party leader with the largest popular vote in the Labour Party's history, there has been a renaissance in activism. This small volume is intended to help activists understand the struggles, defeats and victories of the past.

I have tried to put together an undogmatic easy-to-read abridged history of the British Labour Party, Trade Unions and Labour Movement, drawing on my experience of over 40 years teaching labour and socialist history to trade union shop stewards, conveners and workplace reps.

As Director of the National Museum of Labour History for some 15 years, I had the privilege of meeting trade union and Labour Party leaders both on a professional and personal level, giving me a great insight into what goes on politically behind closed doors. I've researched at great length the history of the Labour Movement, and some of the private papers I have been privy to have not yet been made public.

Unfortunately, because of political prejudice over the last two decades Labour history in any meaningful sense has ceased to be part of the school curriculum and is a minority study in universities – not that we wish to return to the halcyon days of the '60's and '70's, where Labour History became a fashion item interpreted by the middle classes in their own image and with their own values.

There is still so much research needed in the field of Labour history especially the crucial role of women in the Trades and Labour movement, much of which hasn't been fully researched or written about. It wasn't until 2009 that we learned the truth about the Matchwomen's strike of 1888 which launched the new union movement when Dr Louise Raw wrote her ground-breaking book 'Striking a Light'.

Labour historians should learn from the Labour Colleges, the plebs league and all those great Labour and socialist historians who taught and published labour and social history as part of the class struggle, and in some cases were victimised for doing so.

Terry McCarthy

March 2017

Part I

Industry and Empire

The industrial revolution did not happen in a vacuum. We must go back in history to understand the conditions that led to the development of trade and industrialisation in the United Kingdom.

The Reformation broke the dominance of wealth through land value; the new ideology made it easier for merchants to develop trade. Expansion of Empire in the Elizabethan period, especially the slave trade, brought great wealth to the British nation.

New ideas on trade and investment by Oliver Cromwell's Government allowed free trade in money as well as goods. Cromwell's government allowed foreign merchants, including Jews (who were previously barred) and others to trade and reside in Britain. By the seventeenth-century the merchant class had gained the ascendancy - this was a demonstrated fully by the so-called bourgeois revolution of 1688 when the merchant class caused the abdication of the monarch without civil war. In 1694, a private company, the Bank of England, was underwritten by the British state. Previously, the Dutch had tried to launch a similar usury note but did not have the military power to enforce their financial mandates.

Britain became the first modern nation state to have a usury, or banknote, acceptable to other nation states. Britain soon became the centre for the world of banking, insurance and financial services. In a sense Britain became a monetarist nation before it became an industrial one.

Britain's military power, especially its navy, allowed Britain through its 'front' organizations, the West and East India companies, to dominate the slave and opium trades. Farmers in the Indian subcontinent were forced to turn away from agriculture to grow opium, which was then exported to China.

The Emperor of China tried to stem the flood of opium into the country, but the British government interpreted this as an act of war and launched the opium wars 1839-42. The British gained a military victory, also taking control of areas of China such as Hong Kong, and the trade flourished. This oppression made Britain the world's wealthiest nation. With the expansion of Empire, Britain imposed imperial preference - that is, Britain determined the price of raw materials from the Empire and set the price to be paid for finished goods manufactured in the United Kingdom; no other nation state could trade with the Empire. Britain still paraded herself as a leading civilised cultural nation, therefore it had to rationalise why it was involved in slavery and exploitation. Through its propaganda outlets, such as universities and the church and media, it propagated that Negroes, the Chinese and all other indigenous populations controlled by the Empire were inferior.

This propaganda was repeated during the Irish famine, when food was exported to England from Ireland to control the price of corn. No history of the Labour movement is complete without commenting on the wrongly named Irish famine of the 1840's. The fact is there was no famine - there was a failure of one crop, potatoes, which extended throughout Europe. This drove the price of corn and livestock up. A political decision was made not to give relief to Irish farm workers, and that the export of corn and livestock from Ireland should be increased to meet the demand in the rest of the United Kingdom. The population of Ireland went from 9 million down to 4 million in less than a decade. Millions came to the United Kingdom and they had a profound effect on the development of the Labour and Socialist movement.

The employers and state showed the same callous attitude toward the inhuman conditions that many workers, including women and children, had to endure in factories, where no consideration was given to safety. Workers were told that they were lucky to have employment - the alternative being the harsh workhouse system.

The state rationalised this ideology by using the pseudoscience of social Darwinism, claiming those who went for relief were social inadequates and therefore should be punished harshly, and that in this new industrial society, those that were morally superior would rise to the top: there should be a great differential in society to set an example for the poor to work hard and improve their situation.

Britain had total hegemony over markets in its Empire: they determined what crops were to be grown, in many instances forcing cash crops such as opium to be harvested in place of staple crops and closing any embryonic manufacturing, especially in the field of cotton.

We now had a situation where a small nation state, the United Kingdom, had the monopoly on trade and commerce and the largest empire the world had ever seen (a third of the Earth), the problem was that there were no major manufacturing centres in the United Kingdom that had the technology to meet growing demand. The downside of imperial preference was that once you could meet the demand of your market in terms of manufacture, there was no need for research and development.

To beat the tariffs, foreign competition had to produce better machine tools and manufactured goods. From 1850 onwards America and Germany became home to modern inventions, but the British manufacturing class saw no need to educate the workforce, especially in technical education. Ironically, the

14

monies that should have gone on research and development went instead into investing in the industrialisation of America, Germany, France and all other potential competitors. UK foreign investment in the years 1815 to 1880 was £100,000,000. About 600,000 skilled workers migrated to Britain's competitors between 1815 to 1900.

Industrialisation

Manufacturing in the 17th century had hardly changed over the last hundred years; the 18th century however, saw the greatest development of machine and fishing tools. Manufacturers could clearly see that investment in research and development could be recouped a thousand times, so we see the development of the infrastructure through roads railways and canals for the transport of goods and services.

The one commodity that was missing was the large numbers of skilled workers needed to operate the new machines. Britain was still an agricultural nation – manufacturers and bankers had a great deal of wealth but political power, such as seats in parliament, was still based on land wealth.

A struggle now develops between that those who owned the land and those whose wealth came from manufacturing or banking. Manufacturers wanted the free movement of labour so they could recruit people to work in factories whereas landowners wanted their workers to stay on the land.

Due to increased demand the value of land rose; the response from the state was to privatise common land through the Enclosures Act 1770-1820.

Reform

The British state became paranoid following the American Revolution (1776) and the French Revolution (1789). The idea that all men were equal was an anathema to them. Unfortunately for them skilled workers who could read were often keen followers of radicals such as Tom Paine, whose book, The Rights of Man (1791), was thought to be seditious. It became increasingly obvious to those involved in manufacturing and commerce that there had to be radical changes in society to meet their needs for markets and political power.

The conflict of interest between the landowners and the industrialists came to a head in Manchester. Although a major city in terms of manufacturing, mining and banking, Manchester had no parliamentary representation. As a result, an unlikely alliance formed between the radicals of the labour movement and the manufacturing sector, who embraced the idea of American-style democracy.

A crowd of 80,000 had gathered in St Peter's Field, Manchester, to demand the reform of Parliamentary representation. The local mounted yeomanry, under the control of the landowner magistrates, charged the crowd killing 11 - this incident became known as the Peterloo massacre.

Market forces determined that those workers from the old guilds who were numerate and literate were in a very strong bargaining situation when it came to terms and conditions. 40% of men were literate and 25% of women in this period (all classes). The tradition of the old guilds to meet and combine their ideas and experiences to improve their condition worried the authorities. The London Corresponding Society was formed in 1792, strengthening the embryonic trade union movement. Still working outside the law, they began to recruit semi-skilled workers. Many of them went under the banner of the Grand Consolidation of Trade Unions, but an employers' offensive, with help from the state, smashed this initiative.

Such was the concern of the authorities that anti-combination acts were passed in 1799, with the maximum sentences of death or deportation.

As machines took over from unskilled labour, unemployment became rife. Angry workers, known as the Luddites, began to smash machines and burn down factories. The Speenhamland system of payments both to the unemployed and those on very low incomes was introduced in an attempt to quell unrest. This acted as a catalyst for change and 1819 saw the first Factory Act.

The new manufacturing and industrial classes needed labour, whereas landowners needed to keep their labourers. The gap between these two groups became wider as the international democratic revolution spread. Pressure from the industrialists and radicals saw the repeal of the Combination Acts in 1824 but a year later they were made less liberal.

Not that trade unionism was confined to industry: there were riots and industrial action by agricultural workers for better terms, and combinations were being formed. The landowners reacted violently, and in 1834 the Tolpuddle martyrs, agricultural workers who tried to form a union, were indicted, found guilty and transported. There were mass demonstrations over the convictions. The martyrs were later pardoned and allowed to return to their homes, they became a symbol of the struggle against oppression.

To counter trade unionism, the employers brought out the so-called 'document' where workers had to sign a legal document

18

stating that they would never join a trade union. Failure to sign meant they would be put on a blacklist published and distributed to other employers.

Women workers were involved in industrial action, although barred from the main journeyman skilled unions. Despite this there were several strikes during this period such as the Women Bible Workers (the Victorians felt it was their duty to Christianise those in the Empire, millions of Bibles were produced for missionary societies) who had successful strikes in the 1840's and 50's. Although the journeyman printers supported their action, they still barred them from membership.

Women also took industrial action in the tailoring, pottery and cigar-making trades. Much of the industrial action taken by women in this period still hasn't been researched or written about.

Challenge

A combination of political radicals and trade unionists formed the Chartist movement of the 1840's. Chartism was to lay down the foundations of the modern labour movement. There were two distinct schools of thought that came out of Chartism, termed the moral and the physical; 'moral' meaning to work for reform through peaceful campaigning, demonstration and education, rejecting physical violence and 'physical' the belief that the state had to be literally smashed and rebuilt to serve the working class. Chartism should not be dismissed because its call for a general strike and a revolution got little response.

 The Chartist campaign did much in organising those workers who were not unionised. Their demonstrations were massive and, as many of the working class were illiterate, a necessary visible show of the strength of the emerging organised labour movement.

Chartism was a good recruiting sergeant, instructing uneducated people in how to campaign, organise, run meetings and all the mundane things that need to be done before movements and parties can be formed. A point often overlooked in relation to the Chartist movement is that both wings of Chartism were led by Irishmen: O'Connor and O'Brien.

The People's Charter called for six reforms:

- A vote for every man twenty-one years of age, of sound mind, and not undergoing punishment for a crime.

- The secret ballot to protect the elector in the exercise of his vote.

- No property qualification for Members of Parliament in order to allow the constituencies to return the man of their choice.

- Payment of Members, enabling tradesmen, working men, or other persons of modest means to leave or interrupt their livelihood to attend to the interests of the nation.

- Equal constituencies, securing the same amount of representation for the same number of electors, instead of allowing less populous constituencies to have as much or more weight than larger ones.

- Annual Parliamentary elections, thus presenting the most effectual check to bribery and intimidation, since no purse could buy a constituency under a system of universal manhood suffrage in each twelve-month period.

New Model Unions

The repeal of the Corn Laws in 1846 signaled the final victory of the manufacturers and merchants over the land owners, after which the former group felt secure enough to grant reforms such as the Ten Hours Act in 1847, which the emerging Labour Movement had been campaigning and demonstrating for.

Aldgate, East London, 1851, saw the formation of the Amalgamated Society of Engineers. This was the birth of the modern trade union Movement. In 1852, the London Trades Council was formed, followed by the Carpenters and then in 1863 the founding of the Co-operative Wholesale Society. The 1867 Reform Act for the first time allowed working-class men, mainly the skilled, to have a vote and a voice in politics.

In 1868 the TUC was formed in Princes Street, Manchester. It called for the 8-hour day, the repeal of anti-trade union legislation and an extension of the franchise.

The movement had campaigned for some time for universal primary education. This was a granted in 1870, but fell well short of the education being offered to children in France, Germany and America. This failure to understand the importance of education would come back to haunt the ruling class.

The movement also had victories in the 1870's with reforms as diverse as the Plimsoll line, the Coalmines Act and permitted hours of work. This period also witnessed the unionisation of the railways and elements of white collar workers. Joseph Arch established the Agricultural Workers Union in 1872 with the support of Catholic primate Cardinal Manning.

By the 1870's immigrant workers began to organise. The Irish Republican Brotherhood had offshoot unions both in East London and Liverpool. The Stevedores Union was formed in East London in 1871 and was active both in east and southeast London. Exclusively Catholic, it was the first Dockers union to be formed in the United Kingdom. The Miners' Federation was formed in 1880. Jewish immigrants, mainly from Eastern Europe, also formed their own unions in the bakery and clothing trades. They brought with them an understanding of modern European Socialism, both anarchic and Marxist. In fact, the first Marxist papers were published in the 1870's in Yiddish.

The New Union Movement

The importance of the New Union Movement cannot be underestimated. It wasn't just a reaction to bad employers but also to the conservatism of the skilled workers who had dominated the trade union movement through the ineffective TUC. New unionism gave a voice to those who had no say in society. The so-called unskilled workers had been kept at arm's length by the TUC, and if ever there was a movement that sprang from the rank-and-file, new unionism was just that.

There had been talk throughout the decade about organisation both in east and southeast London but it was left to the match workers of Bryant and May in 1888 to fire the first shots against unscrupulous employers and the conservatism of the Labour movement. Match workers were predominantly female and there was a large army of outworkers employed through unscrupulous sub-contractors. It was thought that the workers were impossible to organise, especially the women, although they had managed disputes in the past.

This was a view shared not only by the employers but the Labour movement generally, so it came as a great surprise when the match workers' strike took place.

Work in the match factory was not anyone's first choice. All workers men, women, boys and girls – were aware of industrial diseases such as fosse jaw, and other dangers including explosions and toxic fumes. Matchwomen were considered to be at the bottom of the heap in terms of employment, even amongst the unskilled.

The Matchwomens' action got maximum publicity, enjoying the support of papers like the Times. Sadly, many commentators

24

could not accept that the women won this great victory on their own and have suggested absurdly that the strike was won by a middle-class supporter, Annie Besant (this misinterpretation of history carries on until the present day).

Other women active in the New Union Movement included the Scottish Christian Socialist sisters Margaret and Rachel McMillan, who ran evening classes for working girls in the Docklands and assisted with welfare during the great unrest of 1888-9. Eleanor Marx was also very active, amongst many other things teaching Will Thorne to read and write.

Following on the heels of the Matchwomen, the Gas workers, led by Will Thorne, came out on successful strike and in turn all of the new unions were in dispute with their employers.

In the London Docklands, Tom Mann and John Burns oversaw the formation of the Dockers union assisting Ben Tillet to become leader (although Tom Mann had misgivings). Tom McCarthy, secretary of the stevedores union, was co-opted because he was felt to be a safe pair of hands as well as being a good orator, and, importantly, he had strong links with Dockers on the south side of the river.

No time was wasted in organising and calling for a strike over pay, conditions and recognition. Stevedores joined forces with lightermen and other skilled workers on both sides of the river when the strike was called.

The Dock strike involved thousands, with huge demonstrations, and caught the imagination of the country. The strike was greatly helped by the financial contribution of Australian workers – that small workforce contributed the equivalent of over £1m in today's currency. The nation was divided down the middle. The strike leaders used shrewd tactics to win over the general public:

there was no violence, Rule Britannia not the red flag, no slogans about overthrowing the state. Cardinal Manning acted as arbitrator, and after six weeks of strike the Dockers won recognition and a rise in their hourly rate.

The New Union Movement swept through the whole of Britain: Gas workers, dockworkers, match workers, electricians, builders, printers, paper hangers and box makers, carters, construction workers and many more organised themselves into unions.

The movement did not only pose a problem for employers. The make-up of the TUC, which had been predominantly skilled workers, was drastically changed by the rise in unskilled members, as was its policy toward the state, especially the Liberal Party; there were now calls for a political party to represent organised Labour.

The employers did not take this militancy lying down. From 1890 onwards, with the help of the state, the aim of the right was to break the power of organised Labour.

Socialism

A socialist Labour Party was established in Scotland a decade before the rest of the United Kingdom: 1889 saw the foundation of the Scottish Labour Party. However, there were other non-Labour Party socialist organisations pre-dating this. 1881 saw the foundation of the Social Democratic Federation, a small Marxist party with his own paper, Justice. The Fabian Society was formed in 1883 and the Socialist League, run by William Morris, was founded by resigned SDF members in late 1884.

The Independent Labour Party was founded in Bradford in 1893 by a group of socialist trade unionists, mainly from the north of England. The meeting was led by James Keir Hardie of the Ayrshire miners, and its aim was to draw the trade union movement into an alliance with socialism.

This alliance happened formally when the Labour Representation Committee was founded in 1900, however, not without division among some of the trade union leaders. John Burns, who had been a leading figure in the new union movement, still wanted to continue working with the Liberal Party and did not see the need for a new party at all. From its very foundation there were obvious political contradictions - on one hand you had out-and-out socialists like Keir Hardie, and on the other Fabian reformers such as Bernard Shaw. The divisions became even wider when Tom Mann became ILP secretary in 1894, as both the Fabians and the anglo-marxist SDF refused future affiliation (Beatrice Webb denounced the ILP as a 'wrecking party', however, she also stated that she thought that ILP middle-class supporters were 'not too bright' and many of the working class members were 'stupid').

The emergence of newspapers such as the ILP's own Clarion, and the Pall Mall Gazette under Steadman, had a profound effect, especially in the propaganda war that was going on between the employers and the unions.

It would be wrong to state that there was any great mass movement of socialists or Marxists during this period, despite the fact that both Marx and Engels lived in Britain. There was a great deal of effort to develop a socialist movement on the European scale, but it never appeared. Engels stated that apart from one or two distinguished comrades, such as Eleanor Marx and Tom Mann, there was no appetite amongst the Labour leadership to embrace or understand Marxist or Socialist philosophy, the shadow of Empire seems to obliterate it. Engels said the trouble with the establishment in the British trade union movement is they would rather be in the Mansion House dining with the Lord Mayor than outside demonstrating against it.

In the period before the first World War, only two great thinkers and Marxist activists came from the UK, namely Tom Mann and James Connolly. It was not until 1920 that conditions were right to form a British Communist party which was very influential in the trade union movement. The authorities were so secure in their belief that Marxism hadn't a cohesive base in the UK that they allowed Lenin to live and work in the country.

In the 1895 general election the Independent Labour Party put up 28 candidates, winning 44,325 votes (at this time women and large sections of the unskilled male population were disenfranchised).

In 1900, the Independent Labour Party, the Fabians, and the Social Democratic Federation met with the trade unions in London to form the Labour Representation Committee, with the aim to '*elect working-class men to Parliament to represent the trade unions*

28

and the working-class and to establish a distinct Labour group in Parliament, who would have their own whips and agree their own policy, which must embrace a readiness to cooperate with any party which for the time being may be engaged in promoting legislation in the direct interests of Labour'.

One member from the Fabians, two from the parties and seven members from the trade union movement were elected to run for the LRC. In the 1900 general election the LRC won 62,698 votes. Two other candidates, Keir Hardie and Richard Bell, won seats in the House of Commons.

In 1900 the employers, with help from their allies in Parliament and the courts saw the passing of the Taff Vale judgement. The Taff Vale railway company sued the amalgamated society of railway servants for losses during a strike in 1901 the railway union was deemed to be liable for damages and losses incurred by the employer the union was fined with costs £43,000 which in 2017 values would be the equivalent of £4.85.000. This action was clearly undertaken to destroy the trade union movement. The trade unions responded by lobbying for representation in the House of Commons.

Socialist parties had seats in Parliament before 1900. By 1881, three independent socialist candidates had won seats to the House of Commons; remarkable when remembering that women did not have the vote, and in urban areas up to 40% of working men were also denied the vote. The 1910 general election saw 40 Labour MPs elected.

There were scarcely any official Labour Party constituency organisations (except for those provided by local trade's councils, groups of miners' lodges, and local branches of the ILP). In 1914 there were only two constituency associations with individual members: Woolwich and Barnard Castle, which Will Crooks and

Arthur Henderson had built up on their own, and which of course they used as a power base.

The general election of 1906 saw the election of 30 members of Parliament from the LRC. The elected members assumed the title of 'Labour Party' and elected their first officers and whips. Policy was determined by the Labour Party through the annual conference and its executive authority, the National Executive Committee. There was no official party leader, but an annually elected chairman of the parliamentary party. The Labour Party was still a coalition of socialists although there was no real definition of what this meant in policy terms.

After the 1906 General Election, because of the Lib-Lab pact, the Liberal Government passed the Trades Disputes Act 1906 which removed trade union liability for damage by strike action.

At first glance it would appear that the Liberal Party were the winners of the 1906 election but the Labour Party gained support, especially over its fight against anti-trade union legislation and for social reform. Even the strongest supporters of the Lib-Lab pact began to contemplate a Labour Party independent of any other parliamentary party.

The establishment was not going to sit idly by and watch trade-union sponsored MPs filling the benches of Westminster. In 1908, Mr. W V Osborne, secretary of the Walthamstow Branch of the Amalgamated Society of Railway Servants, claimed that it was illegal for the ASRS to impose a 'political' levy on its members for the support of its sponsored candidates who were elected to parliament. Osborne initially lost his action but Mr Justice Neville's decision was later reversed by the House of Lords. This piece of anti-trade-union legislation was not repealed until 1913.

Rebellion and Reaction

The period before the 1914-18 war is sometimes referred to as the Syndicalist period but apart from Tom Mann of the engineers, there seems to have been little ideology but much action. Syndicalism as a term has meaning in France in two ways: one, as simple unionism and the other, as the revolutionary program for Anarcho-Syndicalism. Syndicalism in Britain as a political theory never had a great ideological base. Tom Mann hero of the new union movement was seen to be the leader of syndicalism man had travelled the world involving himself in disputes in Australia South Africa and America in America he joined up with the Wobblies (the Industrial Workers of the World).

Following a strike by printers who had publicised their dispute by printing a broadsheet entitled The World the trade union movement decided they had to have a daily paper of their own. The Daily Herald came into being in 1912. Labour now had a popular daily paper with a circulation of 25,000. Will Dyson, regarded by many as the greatest cartoonist, was engaged creating cartoons, artwork and posters for the movement. Ben Tillett and the right in the Labour movement were at first very supportive of the paper, until it became the voice of the left supporting Socialism the Labour Party and Industrial action. Tragically the Daily Herald would eventually end up as the right-wing Sun newspaper.

The Transport Strike of 1911 saw Dockers and Transport workers involved in violent conflict throughout the United Kingdom. Police and army retaliation was harsh, especially in Liverpool and Clydeside, and the numbers of trades disputes, ranging from miners to engineers, equaled those of the New Union Movement. Perhaps the most important of these was the

31

Dublin transport strike which lasted for many months. The defeat of that strike not only set back the Irish Labour Movement decades but also enabled Sinn Fein to fill the vacuum by exploiting the fact that the TUC had turned on James Larkin and the Irish Transport and General Workers' Union, denying them secondary action and financial aid.

The Dublin transport strike, which lasted for a year, saw police riots, workers homes invaded, furniture smashed and tenants assaulted, including women and elderly people. The striking workers suffered fatalities, in violence towards workers the like of which had not been witnessed for decades. The defeat of the strike not only set back the Irish Labour movement for decades but it also enabled Sinn Fein to fill the vacuum. Sinn Fein exploited the fact that the TUC abandoned the strikers

There had been great hostility against James Larkin, the charismatic leader and founder of the Irish Transport and General Workers' Union. James Sexton, leader of the Dockers' Union, had successfully prosecuted Larkin for poaching members and funds to set up the ITUWU. Larkin served a short prison sentence, but his union prospered. Larkin and Sexton had totally different political views. Sexton's was on the right of the moment whereas Larkin was very much on the left - as soon as a strike began, he contacted Tom Mann and his allies to help in the conflict.

What terrified the TUC General Council, who had first publicly supported the transport strike, was that the visiting delegation was asked to inspect the Irish citizen's army, which was a military offshoot of the union. The TUC delegates were speechless when they saw ranks of uniformed armed men and women. Not only did they abandon the strike they also personally attacked James Larkin and his allies James Connolly and sister Delia Larkin, who had set up the Irish Women's Workers Union.
32

The defeat of the strike caused a vacuum which was filled by Sinn Fein, a small group that used what they described as 'the betrayal of the British Labour movement' to build a base amongst the working class.

The National Federation of Women Workers was formed in 1906 by Mary Macarthur. By 1914 it had over 20,000 members. Women had been in the forefront of industrial action before the First World War, especially in the numerous factories that had sprung up to meet growing consumer markets, as well as making component parts for industry.

The First World War totally split the Labour movement. Many on the left saw it as an imperialist war, but they were in the minority. The Fabians were very much in favour, whereas the Independent Labour Party was totally opposed. The anglo-marxist Social Democratic Federation was also divided over the war - its leader H. M. Hyndman being in favour (his imperialist jingoism was second to none). ILP member Ramsay MacDonald resigned as chairman of the parliamentary party, with Arthur Henderson succeeding him. Fortunately, due to the federal structure of the Labour Party, McDonald was able to keep his seat on the party's national executive. The right-wing, using jingoism, consolidated their power base in the party machine.

The 1916 Labour Party conference were strongly pro-war supporting conscription. Tom Mann labelled the Fabians 'Lloyd George's poodles'. Lloyd George was indeed thankful, and at every opportunity he praised the patriotism of the Labour Party.

The TUC abandoned strike action for the duration of the war, although the rank-and-file often ignored this dictate despite the ban. The Labour movement made gains on the home front, in the coal mines and in engineering, and there was recognition that women had been an important component of industry since the

33

industrial revolution. Women were encouraged to go into factories to help in the war effort industry.

During the First World War, industrialists made huge fortunes. In spite of this they were forever trying to erode the terms and conditions won by organised Labour production and so profit rose enormously, unlike wages and salaries. Parliament had passed laws outlawing strikes during wartime, nevertheless as early as 1915 the South Miners withdrew their Labour succeeding in their unlawful strike.

The state was in a dilemma to make profits, larger factory units employing sometimes thousands of men and women became commonplace. Union activists took advantage of this, not only unionising the workplaces but politicising the workers as well. So the state began to attack leading militants such as Tom Mann were being prosecuted for their open hostility to the war, expressed in speeches and socialist publications, the Tory press wasted no time vilifying Labour Party members such as Keir Hardie and George Lansbury, declaring them traitors and calling for their prosecution for treason.

One of the most shameful episodes of this period was when Ben Tillet and Horatio Bottomley, who was later convicted of fraud, blackmailed Victor Grayson over his homosexuality; Grayson was married at this time with a daughter. Grayson enlisted in a new Zealand Regiment and was wounded leaving the Army in 1918. Grayson was provided with a luxury flat and given a generous allowance overseen by Maundy Gregory who had masterminded the selling of honours for Lloyd George. Gregory had links to the intelligence service and had a track record of recruiting disillusioned former socialists to denounce the socialist cause.

Gregory met frequently with Ben Tillet and Herbert Morrison. Without their knowledge, Tillets daughter, Jennie, kept Tom Mann informed about the meetings. Grayson through Jennie still corresponded with Tom Mann eventually Grayson was smuggled to Ireland by Tom Mann and James Larkin. Later he moved back to England (I was presented with the correspondence which they used to blackmail Grayson when I was the director of the National Museum of Labour History - the documents had ended up in the possession of JH Thomas, the former railway workers union leader who joined Ramsay MacDonald's national government. Jennie Tillet enjoyed a close personal relationship with Tom Mann which was kept secret from her father, as were her politics, she had hoped to become a musician but her father insisted that she worked in the Dockers union office in East London giving her a pearl handled 32 calibre pistol for her protection).

In August 1914 the parliamentary Labour Party voted to support the government's request for war credits of £100 million. MacDonald resigned as chairman of the party. Arthur Henderson was voted in as party leader Henderson got his reward in May 1915 he became the first member of the Labour Party to hold a Cabinet post when Herbert Asquith invited him to join his coalition government.

The Russian revolution had shaken the establishment throughout Europe and America and socialism and communism were gaining footholds in the Labour movement much to the consolation of people like Ben Tillett and Arthur Henderson and of course the TUC.

The Russian revolution in 1917 split the Labour movement between those on the left who supported the revolution and those on the right that were imposed especially when the Bolsheviks took power. The left mounted demonstrations in

35

support of the revolution. Their anger was intensified with the so-called wars of intervention in 1918, when a combined Allied Force made up for Britain and America, Japan and others, invaded Russia in support of the Russian anti-revolution, pro-Czarists. The intervention failed. European monarchy disintegrated, there was revolution in Germany and elsewhere, the thought of millions of soldiers returning to Britain sent shock waves through the establishment. The British monarchy was so alarmed after 1917 that it refused to give sanctuary to the Czar and is family.

Elements of the right in the Labour Party recognised there had to be a method to contain Bolshevism.to the delight of the left-wing, Sidney Webb and Arthur Henderson came up with Clause IV Part 4: To secure for the workers by hand or brain the full fruits of their industry and the most equitable distribution thereof that may be possible upon the basis of the common ownership of the means of production, distribution, and exchange and the best obtainable system of popular administration and control of each industry or service which they claimed would bring about a social revolution through parliamentary democracy

The leadership of some of the unions were getting concerned that the rank-and-file shop stewards' movement, started on Clydeside in Scotland, was now spreading throughout the country.

1918 witnessed the birth of the modern Labour Party. It totally reorganised itself, adopting a new constitution, including Clause IV.

Following the First World War, all men over the age of 21 were given the vote, it was not until the Equal Franchise Act of 1928 that women over 21 were able to vote, finally achieved the same voting rights as men. Unfortunately, the Equal Franchise Act did

36

not eliminate all franchise inequality: some privileged members of society, such as owners of certain businesses, still had two votes, right up until Attlee.

Employer's offensive

With the end of the War, the boom which occurred because of War-economics soon evaporated. The employers' answer to this was to revert to 1913-14 terms conditions and wage rates. When the workforce resisted, the employers resorted to lockouts in mining, engineering, printing, and every other workplace that refused to accept these conditions. At the end of the First World War the mine owners imposed wage cuts, worsening conditions and exacerbating the problem of non-recognition of unions.

 In 1921 the TUC replaced the parliamentary committee by a new General Council with greater powers; there was disquiet within the left over this move they warned this move took away the power from the rank-and-file. In 1925 the employers demanded more cuts in wages and a longer working week. Negotiations lasted till 1926 when, because of the attitude of the employers, the miners were forced into industrial action under the slogan 'not a penny off the pay or an hour on the day'. Workers the length and breadth of the country came out in solidarity and a general strike was called by the TUC, on condition that they controlled the strike.

The employers and government recruited strike-breakers, including the armed forces. Confrontation seemed inevitable. The TUC weighed up the situation, lost its nerve and called the strike off on its ninth day, although the numbers of strikers on that day were greater than those on day one. Miners who continued alone at risk of starvation felt they would never trust the TUC again.

The miners fought their dispute alone and were forced to capitulate, unemployment was now escalating. The miners' defeat

38

was followed by the defeat of the engineers, wage cuts were now commonplace and trade union membership plummeted. The mine owners imposed harsh conditions which culminated in the general strike of 1926, after mine owners imposed even more wage cuts.

Workers rallied to the defence of the miners. Railway workers, Engineers, Transport and Factory workers all downed tools in support of the miners. The TUC took control. The army now assisted the police and middle-class volunteers, who violently broke up picket lines. The workers retaliated, which sent shudders down the backs of the General Council of the TUC. The TUC general secretary at the time, Walter Citrine, explained to me many years later that the strike had to be called off because there was revolution in the air, a revolution he claimed the workers didn't really want and one that they would lose. So, the strike was called off after nine days, even though there were more people on strike then than at any time during the dispute. The general strike split the trade union movement and the Labour Party.

In 1927 the Tory government passed Draconian anti-trade union laws, Britain entered into recession and the state, as always, turned to austerity. The trade union movement had to consolidate after its losses, and a series of conferences and meetings resulted in the so called 'Bridlington Agreement', whereby unions would no longer poach each other's members and disputes would be settled by the General Council of the TUC. Resolutions were passed at the Labour Party conference stating that once Labour was back in power there would be reforms in trade union law: the movement would have to wait until the election of the Attlee government in 1945 for these to be repealed.

The Communist Party sought a merger with the Labour Party, or dual membership. Herbert Morrison rejected this out of hand, citing Lenin's pamphlet to Sylvia Pankhurst, left-wing Communism and infantile disorder, and other treatises written about the British Labour movement, where Lenin had advocated working through the Labour Party. The CP offered a similar agreement with the Labour Party in 1945 but Herbert Morrison vigorously campaigned not to accept and there was no merger.

There was mass unemployment and the only answer on offer was austerity. Clement Attlee leader of the Labour Party called in vain for Keynesian economics to be employed. The unemployed organised themselves and there were great marches, from Jarrow and South Wales to Parliament to no avail: Chancellor Neville Chamberlain said he was sorry for the unemployed, but that austerity was the only answer.

As the war clouds loomed, Britain began to rearm. Suddenly there was money available. Ship workers on Clydeside and Jarrow were taken back, as were workers throughout the country. The mines became busy again, and when the war started there was a shortage of Labour. Single women were called up, the factories were humming. Ship workers who had been laid-off for so long were incensed when they were accused of being unpatriotic when they wouldn't work seven days a week. Miners worked long shifts, and they also had to guard the pits as members of the Home Guard. In Kent, miners had had enough. They went on strike even though it was illegal. Women workers became active in the shop stewards' movement and the People's Convention. There were disputes the length and breadth of the country.

Trade union membership increased dramatically, the shop stewards' movement became an important weapon in the workers struggle, so when the war against fascism ended, workers were organised both in the unions and in the rank-and-file. With

40

the repeal by the Attlee government of all anti-trade union legislation, and approval of the 'closed shop', union members felt even stronger.

The first big clash came when skilled women workers were asked to vacate their jobs for soldiers being demobbed, and to retrain them. Workplace crèches were shut, as were as other amenities. Herbert Morrison thought women were too easily swayed by Communists. As several major unions did not have elections for general secretaries and other important posts it was left to unelected general secretaries on the general counsel of the TUC to decide these issues. The TUC accepted proposals to relocate the skilled women to lower paid employment. Much to its shame, the left, with some notable exceptions, accepted this reactionary action. Though not a member of the General Council, Ernie Bevin was still dictating TUC policy. The trade union bureaucrats accepted the power of the rank-and-file movement and left the day-to-day running of industry to them. There was an uneasy peace between the trade union hierarchy and the rank-and-file.

Minority Governments

In the 1923 General Election, Labour won 191 seats. Then, with the prompting of the Labour Party the Wheatley Housing Act was passed with a building programme of 500,000 homes for rent to working-class families.

Although the Tories were in power there was recognition by the establishment that before too long Labour would be the governing party. On 22 January 1924, Ramsay MacDonald went to Buckingham Palace to be appointed Prime Minister of a minority government. He apologised for the singing of The Red Flag and the Marseillaise at a Labour Party celebration rally, and made it crystal clear that as long as he was leader of the Labour Party there would not be a challenge to the establishment. Despite his apologies for the past, the establishment was not going to give him or the Labour party an easy ride.

The Daily Mail published a letter claiming to have come from MI5, who had intercepted a letter written by Zinovieff, head of the Communist International, urging British communists to promote revolution. The Zinovieff letter was published in the newspapers four days before the 1924 General Election and contributed to the defeat of MacDonald. The Conservatives won 412 seats and formed the next government. With his 151 Labour MPs, MacDonald became leader of the opposition. MacDonald would not accept that his move to the right had cost votes. On the contrary, he claimed that Labour's reputation of being a socialist party had cost the party the election. He claimed that if the party failed to convince the electorate that they didn't wish to radically change the status quo, they would never be in power. This of course was in contradiction to Clause IV, which was part of Labour's constitution.

In the 1929 General Election the Labour Party won 288 seats, making it the largest party in the House of Commons. MacDonald became Prime Minister again, but he still had to rely on the support of the Liberals.

The election coincided with the Wall Street Crash. Since the end of the First World War the USA had been far and away the richest nation in the world, holding most of the world's gold reserves. Now, events there plunged Britain, and the rest of Europe, into recession and mass unemployment, followed by an economic depression.

MacDonald rejected the economic advice of Keynes. Instead he put forward the idea that there should be cuts in all public expenditure, especially unemployment and other social welfare. His policy was rejected by the majority of his cabinet and party. MacDonald would not accept this and had talks with the Conservatives and Liberals to form a national government, which he did in 1931. MacDonald was expelled from the Labour Party. Clement Attlee described MacDonald and the other Labour MPs that followed him as a shop-soiled pack of cards.

On January 1 1930, the Daily Worker was first published. Along with the other Labour publications, there was now a weekly readership of over 250,000 for worker-oriented papers but in the '30's trade union membership fell. The fear of unemployment and the draconian laws passed after the general strike deterred workers from taking up membership.

The '30's also witnessed the rise in fascism, both in Great Britain and the rest of Europe. Oswald Mosley broke away from the Labour Party; first he formed the New Party then the National Union of Fascists.

The Trade Union and Labour Movement organised itself to defeat Mosley and his Blackshirts, a campaign which culminated in the Battle of Cable Street in 1936. Many members of the Labour Movement joined the International Brigade and fought on the side of the Republicans in Spain against Franco's fascists. The right of the Labour Party publicly disapproved of members going to fight on the Republican side.

George Lansbury became leader of the Labour Party in 1932. He hated fascism but as a pacifist he was opposed to using violence against it. When Italy invaded Abyssinia he refused to support the view that the League of Nations should use military force against Mussolini's army. After his pacifist views were defeated at party conference, in 1935 Lansbury resigned and was replaced by Clement Attlee, a close personal friend who, with his quiet academic approach and the lack of fire in his speeches was not thought by all to be leadership material.

Attlee had been a major in the First World War, and had been wounded. His work with the marginalized, especially child poverty in the Docklands had helped shape his beliefs, as had the imprisonment of his brother Tom, who, like Lansbury was an ardent pacifist. Around this time Attlee wrote the pamphlet 'The Social Worker' and later 'The Labour Party in Perspective', which lays out quite succinctly why socialism is the only answer to poverty.

Attlee had lectured at Ruskin College to trade union and socialist students, and he also joined the leftist Independent Labour Party when he was 24 rather than the Fabians, although Sidney Webb had urged him to do so. He was very active, and rejected overtures to join the Anglo-Marxist Social Democratic Federation. Attlee became branch chairman of the Stepney ILP and described himself when canvassing as a socialist. Attlee, typically, was pragmatic about describing what type of socialist he was - he wasn't a communist, but was far more left-wing than many commentators assert.

War

With the outbreak of war in 1939, splits emerged on the left in the Trade Union and Labour Movement. The Communist party deemed the war to be imperialist and stated that workers should not support the war effort. The ruling class was also split between those who supported Lord Halifax, who wished to appease Hitler and make a settlement, and Winston Churchill, who was implacably opposed to Hitler and wanted to continue fighting despite our losses.

One of the main reasons the labour movement supported Churchill in the national wartime government is because they realised that, as Churchill was a member of the Marlborough family, he would bring with him large sections of the establishment especially those who gained their wealth since the 1666 glorious revolution.

Attlee was made Deputy Prime Minister, and other prominent Labour figures like Bevin and Morrison were given leading roles in the government. The Communist Party and its allies came on board when the Soviet Union was invaded in 1941. The Communist Party was very influential in the shop stewards movement that arose during the Second World War, and used its influence to ensure that war production was at its highest level.

The Labour Movement accepted the imposition of Statute 1305, which outlawed industrial action. There were some famous exceptions to this: Kent miners went on strike and were arrested but soon released, and there were several strikes involving women who were conscripted, noticeably in engineering, not just for parity in terms and conditions but ensuring that where factories had not been unionised before, both men and women should get the right rates of pay. By 1944 a third of the civilian population were engaged in war work, including over 7,000,000 women. 430,000 Women were recruited into industry which gave a total female industrial workforce of 650,000.

The People's Convention was very active in factories and other places of employment. It was a grass-roots rank-and-file organisation which fought for equal pay, with women playing a leading role, such as breaking into the London underground and turning them into 24-hour air-raid shelters, forming Shelter committees which organized emergency ration books, rehousing, re-clothing and finding missing persons.

Despite harsh rationing, the Blitz and long hours, production reached an all-time high. Productivity was especially high amongst women workers Trade union membership and influence began to rise again, and by 1943 the Trade Union and Labour Movement had detailed plans for what sort of society they wanted when war ended. Women had played a vital role during the Second World War; without them the war would have been lost: production targets would never have been met, and without the land army the people would not have been fed. Women also played a major role in the armed services, which is why it was unforgivable for the Attlee government to implement the replacement of women workers, especially those in skilled engineering and heavy construction, with returning servicemen. Not that there would not be jobs available - quite the reverse as there was a shortage of Labour. However, women were forced to take lower paid, less skilled employment. This was out and out chauvinism and this insult did not go unnoticed by women in the Trades Union and Labour Movement, although it's been ignored by the majority of Labour historians.

Ernest Bevin, Production Minister and still the governor of the Transport and General Workers union, had stated that it would take at least 2½ women to do one man's work. At the end of the war, production figures showed him to be totally wrong. He conceded, "Well, perhaps some women have shown to be equal with some men," he then added "but personally I don't believe in women working in factories and construction it's all a bit too Soviet".

Harold Wilson, prompted by Barbara Castle, approached Bevin in his guise as Parliamentary Secretary to the Ministry of Works, to see if something could be done, especially in relation to all the workplace childcare facilities which were being shut down. Bevin acted in his usual way, grabbing Wilson by his lapels, pinning him to the wall and telling him in no uncertain terms to not stick his nose in trade union business, coupled with a string of abuse against Barbara Castle, who was one of the brighter 1945 intakes.

Labour wins but USA rules

Labour won a landslide victory in 1945 and immediately transformed British society by nationalising all major industries, giving independence to India and Burma and bringing about major social reforms in housing, education, the environment and the arts.

The major feature of these acts was the formation of the National Health Service. Labour also repealed all of the anti-trade union legislation that had followed the general strike. More than that, unions were given the privilege of a pre-entry closed shop.

The Trade Union movement grew in membership and influence. It was only through the management of Attlee that this mountain of reform legislation got through. From the very early days of his leadership, Attlee insured these reforming policies became party policy At Cabinet there was little or no discussion about the policy Attlee just wanted to know what each department was doing to enact the legislation - it was said of Attlee he would often stay silent when one word would have done. Herbert Morrison, who had stood against Attlee for the leadership, was hostile to Clause IV and tried his best to undermine Attlee personally. Attlee was more than a match for Morrison - using the open dislike of Morrison by Ernie Bevin, he played one off against the other. A Cabinet colleague remarked to Bevin "Morrison is his own worst enemy", Bevin quipped "not while I'm alive".

Some of the things the Attlee government achieved while the country was Bankrupt

- **The National Health Service (NHS)** In 1948 the NHS treated some 8,500,000 dental patients and dispensed more than 5,000,000 pairs of spectacles during its first year of operation. Between 1948–51, Attlee's government increased spending on health from £6,000,000,000 to £11,000,000,000 - an increase of over 80%, and from 2.1% to 3.6% of GDP.

- **Housing** Over 1,000,000 new homes were built to assist home ownership, the limit on the amount of money that people could borrow from their local authority in order to purchase or build a home was raised from £800 to £1,500 in 1945, and to £5,000 in 1949.

- **National Assistance Act** Local authorities had a duty "to provide emergency temporary accommodation for families which become homeless through no fault of their own". Development rights were Comprehensive Development Areas Planning Act, allowed local authorities to acquire property in the designated areas using powers of compulsory purchase in order to re-plan and develop urban areas suffering from urban blight or war damage.

- **Women and children** Introduced universal family allowances Married Women (Restraint upon Anticipation) "to equalise, to render inoperative any restrictions upon anticipation or alienation attached to the enjoyment of property by a woman," Provision of home-helps for nursing and expectant mothers and for mothers with children under the age of five

- **Workers' rights** Sick leave was greatly extended, and sick pay schemes Fair Wages. Workers' Compensation (Supplementation) The Trades Disputes Act 1927 was repealed, and a Dock Labour Scheme was introduced in

1947 to put an end to the casual system of hiring labour in the docks.

- **Agricultural Wages Board** In 1948 not only safeguarded wage levels, and health and safety standards, but also ensured that workers were provided with accommodation.

- The abolishing of hard labour, penal servitude, prison divisions and whipping.

- Nationalisation of the Bank of England, British Electricity Authority, Cable & Wireless, National Rail, Water, Transport, some road haulage, some road passenger transport. Gas supply and the iron and steel industry.

One of the main reasons why the Labour government was defeated in '51 (although getting more of the popular vote than the Tories) was the economic burden that they carried following the Second World War.

The USA demanded that payments on the war debt begin immediately at the end of hostilities, and the terms imposed on the loan were harsh. In addition to loan repayments, the USA demanded access to UK markets in the Commonwealth and old empire, and an end to imperial preference where the USA and its interests were concerned.

The United Kingdom still had a war economy and it was recognised that it would take some time to retool and retrain its workforce. The USA on the other hand had begun to move away from a war economy as early as 1944, and was producing more manufactured goods and white goods than arms by 1945.

Coupled with this was the fact that the USA had demanded that after World War II the dollar would be the supreme currency, that commodities such as gold, silver and oil would have to be paid for in dollars, and that all other currencies would have to relate to the value of the dollar. Congress also demanded that Britain give up its portfolio of USA shares. Britain therefore had to export or die. Rationing became worse after the war than during it.

 There were no resources to research and develop machine tools, and the country suffered a decline in market share because it could not produce the quality or quantity of goods that the USA did. The USA initiated the International Monetary Fund (IMF), which allowed it to open up markets for its manufacturing base.

As the Cold War began the USA was concerned that Europe might go communist. The Marshall Plan was devised to give aid and loans to Europe to minimise the chance of this happening. It did create a breathing space, but the downside was that Germany and Japan were totally re-tooled and their currency was kept artificially low against the dollar, and the USA also opened up its markets to them with generous quotas whilst Britain was left to fend for itself. As a result, within a decade of the ending of the Second World War, West Germany's population enjoyed a higher living standard than that of the UK. Japan soon followed suit ending up as the world's second richest nation, with Germany third, becoming the USA's greatest competitors.

An example of American dominance was the founding of the state of Israel. It took the Conservatives another decade following the Suez fiasco in 1956 to fully understand American hegemony. In the late 1940's America approached Britain calling for a joint working party to enquire into the feasibility of an Israeli state in Palestine which was then under British mandate. Unfortunately the British delegation had not quite come to terms

52

with American hegemony, and the Attlee government argued for a protected Israeli homeland rather than a state.

The British delegation's conclusions were overruled. America agreed that the hundred thousand displaced Jews should be allowed to emigrate to Palestine and that they would support a resolution in the United Nations to bring about the state of Israel. This resolution was also supported by the USSR and the overwhelming majority of UN members (33 in favor, 13 against the resolution). Britain abstained, which brought about some hostility from the political right in Israel and beyond, which lives on to the present day. Dick Crosland, a leading post-war Labour politician, criticised Attlee for not confronting America over the issue more vigorously. Crosland was originally an ardent supporter of the Arab and Palestinian cause, but after meeting Chaim Weizmann, president of Israel, he had a change of heart and declared himself a Zionist.

The Conservative Party had much closer links ideologically with the US administration than did Labour. The USA viewed the Attlee government as too left-wing and it was made clear to the Conservatives that if they did get back into office the terms of the debts would be eased and soft loans would be made available. This allowed the Conservatives to offer the British electorate more consumer goods and an end to rationing but still maintain the health service and all the other reforms that the Labour government had put in place. However, this was done on borrowed money for consumer goods, not on any long-term plan of research and development, and without the technical education that might win back a position as one of the world's innovators of manufactured goods and machine tools.

The 13 years the Conservatives were in power were rightly labelled '13 wasted years' as far as the manufacturing base was concerned. Even after the narrow defeat of Labour in 1951, the trade unions still enjoyed industrial power. The Conservative government had accepted Keynesian economics, full employment and one-nation Toryism. Trade Union membership continued to grow until in the '70's, with over 13 million members - nearly 49% of the workforce.

A House Divided

Hugh Gaitskell became leader of the Labour Party in 1955. A divisive figure, he had entered the '45 parliament as a left-winger and unilateralist. He moved rapidly to the right as Chancellor in 1945-51. He chose to charge for prescriptions, spectacles and dental treatment to pay for the deficit incurred by the Korean War and general rearmament. This caused a major rift with the left. Aneurin Bevan and Harold Wilson both resigned from the Cabinet over this issue.

Gaitskell unsuccessfully tried to change the Labour Party constitution much on the lines of the rejected amendments put forward by Herbert Morrison in the post-war period. However Gaitskell shone in his attacks on the Anglo-French and Israeli intervention to secure the Suez Canal. Gaitskell blamed the left of the party for the election defeat in 1959, and once again tried unsuccessfully to amend Clause IV of the party's constitution.

After 1951 Labour became less radical. The left argued this is why they weren't doing well electorally. Gaitskell took the opposite view: he argued the Labour Party with its working-class image and its close ties to the unions was out of date, as was Clause IV. He argued perhaps we should try to find a compromise with the Liberals.

Gaitskell tried to write Clause IV out of the constitution but this was too far for even his right-wing trade union barons, who he now relied upon to push his centre-right agenda (many of the trade unions then had appointed, not elected, general secretaries often not reflecting the views of their membership. This was one of the main reasons that the shop steward and rank-and-file movement became so powerful, often calling strikes against the wishes of their general secretaries).

The block vote at the Labour Party conference gave trade unions an inbuilt majority. In 1960 individual membership stood at 790,192 whereas trade union affiliated membership was 5,512,688. Frank Cousins, leader of the Transport and General Workers Union, was Gaitskell's nemesis: a unilateralist and a great orator and through and through socialist.

It was Cousins that drove unilateralism to become party policy. Gaitskell had learned one thing from Attlee: that was to control the party; you had to control the machine. He got together a small group of PLP members and right-wing trade union leaders, such as WJ Carron who was the Engineer's leader. This group went under the banner of the Campaign for Democratic socialism. Bit by bit they took control of the machine and they were able to reverse unilateralism as Labour Party policy but they were not strong enough to change the constitution and abandon Clause IV Frank Cousins went on to be a Cabinet minister in Wilson's government which caused consternation in the centre right ranks of the party

Gaitskell had learned one thing from Attlee, that to control the party you had to control the machine. He got together a small group of PLP members and right-wing trade union leaders such as WJ Carron, who was the Engineers' leader. This group went under the banner of the Campaign for Democratic Socialism. Bit by bit they took control of the machine and they were able to reverse unilateralism as Labour Party policy, but they were not strong enough to change the constitution and abandon Clause IV.

When the Labour conference voted in 1960 to become unilateralist, Gaitskell made his famous speech against the decision, stating, "We will fight and fight and fight again for the party I love." With the help of the union barons, Gaitskell and his supporters reversed the decision the following year. He was challenged unsuccessfully for the leadership of the party by Harold Wilson in 1960. Gaitskell was totally opposed to the common market. He died in January 1963, aged 56, and Harold Wilson, supported by the left, won the leadership contest against George Brown and James Callaghan.

A Labour government was returned in 1964. Leader Harold Wilson's intention was to radically change and modernise British society and the governments of 1964-70 achieved much of what they set out to do. However the underlying economic situation remained the same.

Britain was trying to compete in the world manufacturing markets with Germany and Japan, and the emerging Asian nations such as South Korea, all of which had an unfair advantage in terms of the value of their currency.

The Cold War was at its height and the USA was determined that other nation states should see the value of American capitalism demonstrated by the wealth of their friends and allies.

There was much anger in the US administration over the fact that Harold Wilson would not involve British troops in Vietnam, indeed Wilson's foreign and national policy was an incentive for the Federal Bank of America not to help the pound, which Wilson was forced to devalue. Wilson had a very close relationship with the trade union movement – some would say it got too close when Frank Cousins, the general secretary of the Transport and General Workers' Union, was given a parliamentary seat and was made a cabinet member. In 1966 Barbara Castle introduced a White Paper, In Place of Strife, calling for reform in the trade union movement. The unions successfully demanded that there should be no discussion on the issue, and that 'In Place of Strife' should be abandoned.

There were no membership elections for the post of general secretary in many of the General unions such as the Transport and General Workers union, and most of the industrial unrest at this time such as the seamen's strike in 1966 were led by rank-and-file elected shop stewards and conveners. Wilson denounced the seamen's strike, blaming outside communist agitation. He arranged unofficial meetings, over the heads of the TUC, with the strike leaders. The strike was called off following Wilson's intervention, both to the seamen and to the employers, in relation to the seamen's grievances. Wilson was to employ the tactic of unofficial meetings and links with individuals and institutions outside the Labour party with some success.

The Labour government tried to impose wage freezes, and prices and incomes policies, on the Labour Movement. Divisions were caused when the leadership of the unions accepted terms and conditions that seemed unacceptable to the rank and file. Although in the end the policies were abandoned, they were an opportunity to move to a planned economy.

The Wilson governments were limited in terms of finance, although wages and living conditions improved year-on-year. What they did do, in spite of the lack of financial resources, was to totally change the British social landscape. When Harold Wilson became Prime Minister in 1964 human rights activists were initially disappointed at the lack of expected reforms. Wilson had talked of the necessity for great social reform without going into detail, probably because he knew he had to convince elements in the party, especially the trade unions, of the case for such reform.

The decriminalisation of homosexuality was a case in point. A task force was set up to work on the rank-and-file of the unions, convincing them it was right to back such legislation. Individual members of parliament were approached to bring in private

58

members' bills that would be supported by the government. In this instance, Leo Abse introduced the bill. Abortion was another example. This time, David Steel introduced the bill, which was backed by the government and passed successfully.

Wilson ignored opinion polls that stated that the majority were opposed to the abolition of hanging and flogging, and continued the piece-by-piece reforms: rights for women such as equal pay, legalised abortion and the pill; in education, red-brick universities, the Open University and the comprehensive system, ending the compulsory 11-plus exam; then the Race Relations Act, the Gaming Act and an end to censorship in the arts, literature and theatre.

Rank-and-file under attack

Governments, including Labour ones, were concerned by the power of the rank-and-file movement. They had been the most successful in obtaining better terms and conditions for their industries. There was not one industry that didn't benefit from the rank-and-file movement. Sadly, we now know that the liaison committee for the defence of trade unions, the brainchild of Communist Party industrial organiser Bert Ramelson, was infiltrated by informers. The Docks were controlled by various liaison committees, the London Docks liaison committees spokesman Jack Dash ended up on the cover of Time magazine described as an 'enemy of democracy'. The car industry had 'Red Robbo' Derek Robinson. Many other industries had similar charismatic leaders. Jack Dash would always say "dealing with the Port of London authority is easy. Jack Jones [who was general secretary of the Transport and General workers union], that's another matter."

The '60's also saw the re-awakening of the women's movement both on the industrial front with successful strikes for the Equal Pay Act. At Fords Dagenham and in Scotland, radical feminism came to the fore. Students became radicalised and university occupations were commonplace, with students playing a leading role in anti-Vietnam War and CND demonstrations. The Shop Stewards' movement had grown in strength throughout the '60's and '70's.

Often union leaders seemed remote, and as there was no voting for general secretaries, there was a feeling that the leadership didn't represent the rank and file membership. The organisation of the rank and file movement was lead in great part by The Liaison Committee for the defence of trade unions, under the leadership of Bert Ramelson, and the stewardship of Kevin Halpin.

Women were very much to the fore, militants like May Hobs organised industrial action by the night cleaners in the London Shell building and the action soon spread throughout London. A decade later we saw the same rank-and-file organisation 'when Jayaben Desai led the strike at Grunwick Film Processing Laboratories before they'd even joined a union letter strike and organise news without any help from the unions Governments, even Labour ones, were concerned about the rank-and-file movement as they had been the most successful in obtaining better terms and conditions within their industries: there was not one industry that didn't benefit from the rank-and-file movement.

Ballot rigging in the Electricians union was a blow to the reputation of the trade union movement. There was great concern in the dock industry, where many Dockers and Stevedores were concerned and disillusioned by the Jones Aldington agreement: the jobs-for-life agreement was negotiated away, to be replaced by permanent-work status within the docks industry. Many rank-and-file members felt that they had not been consulted fully. The stevedores, who had no full-time officials, were totally opposed to the agreement

The Jones Aldington agreement was one of several examples of the work of a leadership that failed to take note of the new dynamic in capitalism (neo-liberalism) or the views of the membership. Sympathetic economists predicted that the land values in the docklands area, with its potential for development for commercial gain, changed the power balance – but they were ignored or ridiculed. Sadly, their predictions came true. The London Docklands, with all their history of militancy, are now a memory. In their place, the money merchants built cathedrals to monetarism.

 When the Tories introduced the Industrial Relations Act in 1971 there was great opposition, with strikes and huge demonstrations, court injunctions flying about like confetti. Edward Heath and the Tories were humiliated in 1972, when five Dockers and Stevedores, known as the Pentonville Five, defied the law and picketed a container depot. They were arrested and sent to prison. There was a mass outcry and the TUC called a one-day general strike. Millions answered the call and Edward Heath was forced to release the Dockers.

When Margaret Thatcher became leader of the Conservative party she laid plans to defeat organised Labour. In 1980, following further anti-trade union legislation, she began systematically picking off the unions, starting with the miners. She forced the strike by making it public that there would be major mine closures. Arthur Scargill, the miner's leader, called for a strike immediately. Yorkshire came out, so did other pits. Sections of the miners unfortunately believed the propaganda that their pits would be safe from closure.

There was a great deal of support from the rank-and-file, however the anti-Scargill propaganda went into overdrive and eventually the TUC abandoned the strike, as did Neil Kinnock, the leader of the Labour Party, and after a year of struggle, the miners were forced into surrender. The right now turned their attentions to those who had supported the miners, in some cases victimising those working within the movement.

During the strike there had been great violence shown by the police. It was repeated when the print workers were forced into industrial action by Rupert Murdoch, aided and abetted by the state. One by one the most powerful unions were defeated, and

62

the TUC had no answer to this. Unfortunately, at this time the General Secretary of the TUC was Norman Willis, perhaps the most ineffective TUC General Secretary ever.

Unemployment rose, trade union membership fell. There was hope when a Labour government was elected under Tony Blair, but this proved to be a false-dawn. Tony Blair was no friend of the trade unions: his right-hand man Peter Mandelson shared the same anti-trade union sentiments as his grandfather, Herbert Morrison.

Trade unions had been transformed over recent years, becoming more democratic, reflecting the views of their rank-and-file, no longer advocating and endorsing the right in the Labour Party but now openly campaigning for socialism. Hence, they became one of the driving forces behind Jeremy Corbyn's successes.

Fightback

The Conservatives won a narrow victory in 1970. Leader Edward Heath introduced the Industrial Relations Act, intended to reduce the power of the trade unions.

The labour movement responded with massive demonstrations against the Act and there were strikes. These were deemed to be secondary and illegal. The Engineers Union was fined and warned that all of its funds would be seized and frozen if the strikes continued. The strikes were in fact unofficial, and the leadership had little or no control over them. Five East London dockworkers were imprisoned, which led to mass demonstrations and walk outs. An unofficial general strike seemed to be on the cards but Edward Heath relented and the Dockers were released. Joe Gormley, leader of the National Union of Mineworkers, won a successful strike against the government by using modern public relations and insisting that the strike was not about politics or removing governments, and when Edward Heath went to the country on the basis of "Who runs the country?" the public didn't respond as he had hoped.

In February 1974 Labour won a narrow majority, and the October poll strengthened Labour's control only slightly, to a five-seat majority. Despite the difficult political circumstances, the resulting Labour government lasted five years, and managed to pass significant pieces of legislation on health and safety, trade union legislation, and rents. The issue of Europe was resolved with a national referendum in 1975, which supported membership of the Common Market (now the European Union) by two to one.

Wilson was replaced in 1976 by James Callaghan. Callaghan had defeated Michael Foot, the left-wing candidate, for the position.

The Parliamentary Labour Party voted by a small margin for Callaghan, although in the constituencies Foot was the favourite.

In the 1970's, The Organisation of the Petroleum Exporting Countries (OPEC) took full control of the petroleum industries, acquiring the major say in the pricing of crude oil on world markets. On two occasions, oil rose steeply in a volatile market, triggered by the Arab oil embargo in 1973. Capital markets went into sharp recession as a result, leading to high unemployment throughout the Western world.

In 1975 the Treasury informed the UK government that there would be a £4bn deficit by the end of the financial year. Faced with this, the government sought to borrow from the International Monetary Fund. The IMF laid down stringent conditions on the loan, including cuts in welfare benefits. Denis Healey, the Chancellor, was furious when it emerged that the deficit was only £2bn. Callaghan opted for austerity to solve the deficit, which led to unemployment and cuts in welfare. Callaghan lost his majority in the House of Commons, then entered into a Lib-Lab pact which was endorsed by Michael Foot, much to the surprise of the left in the party. Inflation began to fall, interest rates were lowered from the 15% at the height of the crisis, but workers felt aggrieved at pay cuts in real terms.

By the end of the summer of 1976, there had been a run on the pound. The US administration refused to intervene. The British economy had become so weakened that the Labour government had to seek a loan from the International Monetary Fund, accompanied by harsh conditions including deep cuts in public spending. By August 1977, unemployment levels had surpassed 1,600,000. The media had a field day.

Every opportunity was taken to discredit the trade union movement. Unfortunately, they largely succeeded. The movement had not come to terms with the modern media, especially the new ownership of papers like the Sun.

The Labour government ended in crisis, with industrial action throughout the country in 1979, including public sector and local authority workers. There were violent scenes on the picket lines when Asian women workers came out on strike at the Grunwick plant. Miners joined the women on the picket lines. It was branded by the press the 'Winter of Discontent'; Callaghan had rejected devolution referenda in Scotland and Wales which lost the Labour Party much support.

Neo-Liberalism

The Conservatives came back into power in '79 led by Margaret Thatcher. She totally rejected the post-war Conservative ideology of the one-nation state. She also rejected Keynesian economics. Thatcher had a new ideology, Neo-liberalism, which was acceptable to the establishment because they believed that the end of the Cold War would mean an end to major manufacturing production fuelled by the arms industry. Thereafter, an alternative source of wealth-making was to be making money out of money itself. Monetarists saw trade unions as the enemy of economic stability, and their powers were to be curbed at any cost.

The miners' strike, Wapping and all the other disputes of the time were seen as proof that the trade unions were out of date and out of tune with modern society. Under Thatcher surveillance of activists in the Trades and Labour movement went into overdrive: the number of police officers embedded in the movement increased tenfold. The state had concluded it could not allow organised Labour to gain the upper hand as they had done in the '72 and '74 successful miner's strikes where mass picketing was employed. Anti-trade union legislation had seemingly tamed the leadership of the trade unions; this was not the case with the rank-and-file.

The courts were then enlisted to deal with these militants, demonstrated by the case of the six pickets who were charged with conspiracy to intimidate, unlawful assembly and affray in relation to the building industry in 1973, although it became clear from the start that there was no case to answer. Nevertheless, in an obvious miscarriage of justice, Des Warren, Eric Tomlinson and John McKinsie were sentenced to three years, two years and nine months respectively, and three others received suspended sentences. There were other such incidents, and in many cases the 'embedded' police officers were acting as agent provocateurs. The state, along with employers organisations, put together a blacklist of trade union activists: these actions wrecked lives. The state also formed the special patrol group (SPG) on the lines of the Royal Ulster Constabulary - these officers were trained on military lines and carried no number or insignia, patrolling in unmarked vehicles, their brutality and racism resulted in the Brixton riots.

In 1979 Blair Peach, a New Zealand born teacher, was murdered by police in an anti-racist demonstration in Southall. The officers concerned were exposed by the BBC but no prosecutions have ever taken place. The SPG were also employed at the Wapping dispute and in 1986 the SPG violently attacked both demonstrators and the media, in the process wrecking a nearby public house that was used by pickets and sympathisers. Such was the outcry against the SPG they were disbanded in 1987 to be replaced by the Territorial Support Group.

The media also launched an anti-rank-and-file campaign at this time, accusing those that had organised fundraising for the miners' strike 1984 as being in league with the East German secret service, the Murdoch press also launched vicious personal attacks on activists knowing full well that they would not talk to strikebreaking journalists – effectively giving them no right of reply.

The Murdoch press, especially the Sun, become synonymous with sleaze and bigotry and anti-trade unionism - it vilified any industrial action, especially the miners, often publishing false information. It infamously lied about the Hillsborough disaster and was found guilty of phone-hacking, having corrupt links with the police, public officials and politicians. Murdoch's ownership of the paper led directly to the sacking of 5,500 employees.

Members of right-wing unions played a leading part in ensuring that Murdoch could recruit strike breaking Labour: The Sun's sister paper, the Sunday Times, also launched a series of articles attacking not just Trade Union leaders during the Wapping dispute, but individual shop stewards, Fathers and Mothers of Chapel, and union supporters.

Once organised labour was defeated, the state felt safe enough to switch from Keynesian economics to the monetarist theories of Friedrich Hayek and Milton Friedman. The no-such-thing-as-society mentality these theories prescribed led to the sale of council houses and the privatisation of nationalised industries, with a resultant rise in property values. Huge private pensions were promised 'tomorrow'. This was the 'loads-a-money' era. Neo-Liberal dogma saw socialist education, history, and culture as propaganda tools for Marxists. There was a concerted effort to change or destroy these working-class institutions. Unfortunately they were largely successful in their campaign – but not without a fight, and The Morning Star, Britain's only socialist daily paper, survived.

Neo-liberalism states that the quantity of money available in an economy determines value and that increases in the money supply are the main cause of inflation. It attacks legal and other impediments to labour market flexibility; advocates 'reservation wages' the lowest wage for which a person will work; promoting the free market not just for its economic efficiency, but also for its moral strength. The moral superiority of free markets is said to be proven. In a market economy the only way to value any item, including public services, is by its price; this gives incentive to people to create more personal wealth. There must always be a marked differential between rich and poor so that the poor will see the necessity to educate themselves, acquire skills and, thereby, wealth.

But then the consequences began to appear. Under neo-liberalism there was little or no place for manufacturing. Property prices and unemployment were subject to the vagaries of the market. Major cuts in the health service, education and social services caused unrest. People's anger, no longer channelled through the trade union movement, led to riots.

The trade union movement had to go through a profound change. A heart-felt search was on for the necessary reforms: the election of general secretaries, more accountability to the membership (whose concerns tend to be as much about pensions, the environment, sexual politics and other issues as they are about terms and conditions of employment), modern and relevant education, PR techniques and above all, an understanding of what kind of society Britain would be in the 21st century.

Move to the left

Michael Foot became leader of the Labour Party in 1980. Labour MPs elected him in preference to Denis Healey. Foot came from a political family, a socialist from his early days, he was however anti-communist.

After leaving university he became a journalist, working first for the New Statesman and then for the left-wing journal Tribune. He then moved on to the London Evening Standard. In 1945 he moved to the left-wing Daily Herald and in the same year he became a Labour MP, gaining a reputation for backing left-wing causes. He was a founder member of the campaign for nuclear disarmament (CND).

Foot was a great admirer of Aneurin Bevan, but his greatest hero was the 18th century reformer Tom Paine. Foot became a member of 'the awkward brigade', having the whips withdrawn in 1961 because of his opposition to defence spending. He also refused to serve in the Wilson government because of the party's policy towards Vietnam, incomes control and the common market. Along with Peter Shore, Foot led the fight against membership of the European Union.

After his failure to become deputy leader he accepted a post in the 1974 Labour government as Employment Secretary. He had a close relationship with the unions, and was criticised for not standing up to trade union leaders such as Jack Jones.

When Harold Wilson stood down in 1976, Foot was encouraged to stand for the position of leader but was defeated by James Callaghan. When Labour began to lose by-elections, and seemed in danger of losing its parliamentary majority, it was Foot's successful negotiations with David Steel that produced the Lib-Lab pact.

This, however, led to a rift with the left in the party. The left had seen Foot as a chance to restore the Labour Party to their definition of socialism, calling for state ownership and a fundamental change of the rules in the party, especially in relation to the election of the leader. Foot elected for compromise but the issues were too fundamental for any compromise. Right-wing members left to form the Social Democratic Party, while the left was split between the hard-line Trotskyist militant tendency and the traditional Labour Party left.

The left were also disappointed by Foot's wholehearted support for Thatcher's military intervention to win back the Falkland Islands from Argentina; and especially by his attacks on Peter Tatchell. Tatchell had been an active member of Bermondsey Labour Party and was chosen democratically to be the parliamentary candidate for the constituency, but Foot attacked him on the grounds that he had openly supported extra-parliamentary activity. Tatchell, along with other members of the Labour Party, had been very active in the LGBT campaign. The propaganda put out by the Liberal Party was openly homophobic, despite all the efforts of the leadership of the party. Tatchell's constituency party backed him but unfortunately the same couldn't be said for the leadership, who instructed the party machine not to help Tatchell. The seat was won by the Liberals, Michael Foot was attacked viciously by the media, most famously when he wore what they described as a donkey jacket to the Cenotaph commemorations.

Neil Kinnock was first elected to Parliament in 1970. He declared himself to be on the left of the party, a supporter of CND, and opposed to Welsh devolution. James Callaghan appointed him as opposition spokesman on education in 1979.

Much to the annoyance of the right in the party, Kinnock campaigned for more democracy in party leadership elections. He did not support what he perceived to be Michael Foot's wholehearted support for Thatcher's stand on the Falklands War. When Michael Foot resigned as leader, Kinnock was a firm favourite to replace him. Under the new rules, he won 71.27% of the total vote. He enjoyed the support of the left and became leader in 1983. However, it soon became clear that Kinnock's loyalties were with the centre-right of the party. Moving against Tony Benn's attempts to become deputy party leader, Kinnock complained that the rise of the left in the party would be detrimental to election success. He also alienated the left by his attacks on Arthur Scargill and the miners' strike.

There had been a rise of the traditional Labour left, but also that of the Militant Tendency, a hard-left Trotskyist group, which regained control of Liverpool City Council and had influence in many others. There had been as many attacks by Militant on the traditional Labour left as they were on the right of the party however, when it became apparent that the party planned to expel Militant Tendency members, the traditional left defended them. In fact the traditional left had made most gains by unseating militants in many urban constituencies. It was only when, on the eve of the conference, reports came back showing that the Militant Tendency had lost control in many areas that Kinnock decided to make his attack on militants and call for their expulsion, which duly took place.

In 1979, a group of right-wing Labour MPs, Trade Union leaders and activists formed themselves into the St Ermins Group, named after the hotel they had their meetings in. The groups object was to prevent followers of Tony Benn from gaining power at all levels of the party, they were also very active in attacking trade union rank-and-file activity and this included compiling lists of trade union militants. This grouping also went

73

under the name of Labour Solidarity and elements of the group are still active.

At this time, Peter Mandelson took over the party communications department and also began to have a greater say in policy. Labour lost the '87 election and again, the left were blamed. Mandelson put forward the proposition, endorsed by Kinnock, that Clause IV should be dropped and a new set of aims and values introduced. In 1988 Tony Benn challenged Kinnock for the leadership; however the left in the membership was in sharp decline, many being disillusioned by Kinnock especially after he turned against the closed-shop agreements that many unions had with employers. This was seen as an attack on fundamental socialist values. Kinnock won 88.6% of the vote against Benn's 11.4%.

However modernisation did not bring success and in 1992 Labour once again lost the election, this time to John Major, even though the Conservative Party was in disarray and the country longing for change. Kinnock announced his resignation as Labour Party leader on 13th April 1992. He went on to become a European Commissioner, then Vice-President of the European Commission. He became Baron Kinnock in 2005, by this time a millionaire. He also attacked Jeremy Corbyn and the party's move to the left.

John Smith first entered Parliament in 1961. His talents were noted by Harold Wilson, who made him Under-Secretary of State at the Department of Energy. In December 1975, Jim Callaghan promoted him to become Minister of State at the Privy Council office. Unlike Kinnock, Smith was a supporter of devolution and used all his legal skills to successfully follow through the controversial devolution proposals for Wales. Scotland appointed Smith Secretary of State for Trade. In this post, Smith was the youngest member of the cabinet. He was a
74

supporter of the European Community, which alienated his friends on the left, such as Michael Foot.

Smith was however undoubtedly a traditional Labour Party politician. He was an outspoken critic of neo-liberalism, criticising both Nigel Lawson and Sir Alan Walters, who was Mrs Thatcher's economic adviser. Walters was a keen disciple of Milton Friedman and neo-liberal economics. He had also been an adviser to the Chilean dictator Pinochet.

Smith's attacks on neo-liberalism and his support for Keynesian economics did not go down well with Peter Mandelson and Tony Blair. He had come through the grass roots of the party and had a keen understanding of the views and importance of the party membership, and so advocated democratic reforms of the party. He was appointed Shadow Chancellor by Neil Kinnock in July 1987. The right blamed Smith for proposing raising the top rate of income tax from 40p in the pound to 50p, stating it was one of the reasons that Labour lost the 1992 election

He became leader of the Labour Party in July 1992, when he beat Bryan Gould. He won by a large majority in the constituencies and affiliates, but only secured 23.2% of the parliamentary vote. Smith began to re-energise the party machine and membership began to rise. Labour began to do well in local elections and in the opinion polls. He continued to oppose neo-liberalism and supported change in economics.

By the time of his death through a heart attack on 12th May 1994, the Labour party had a professional and modern election strategy and team. The party's popularity with the public had grown exponentially. Internal and external polls showed that if John Smith had been leader Labour would have won the election. John Smith could be said to be the architect of Tony Blair's election victory.

New Labour

The Labour Party was transformed in the 1990's by a small but influential group working under the banner "New Labour, New Party". They believed that Labour's traditional values of nationalisation, Keynesian economics and an ever-closer relationship with the trade unions were the very values that stopped Labour coming into power in a modern age. Frustrated by 18 years of Conservative government, the Labour Party was at its lowest ebb and many, out of a feeling of desperation, voted through the changes including abandoning Clause IV.

Tony Blair, who came from a conservative family, and showed no interest in politics until he became a student at Oxford University, was elected Prime Minister in 1997 with a landslide. Hopes for reform following the Thatcher years had never been higher. However, Tony Blair and his Chancellor Gordon Brown were firm believers in monetarism, both its economic rules and philosophical dogma.

Blair was influenced greatly by Peter Mandelson, who was a keen advocate of Neo-liberalism and a disciple of Freemanite philosophy, believing in capitalist society and that the value of health, medicine, education and the utilities could only be judged by the financial price paid for them. Peter Mandelson dusted down a Labour Party constitution written by his grandfather, Herbert Morrison, which Morrison had tried unsuccessfully to get past the Labour Party conference in the late '40's. The constitution took away the powers from conference and, most importantly, abandoned Clause IV. Blair managed to get the 1931 constitution eradicated to be replaced by the Morrison/Mandelson model. Under the new rules the party headquarters now had powers over local constituencies to install Labour Party parliamentary candidates. In some cases local constituencies were wound up so that candidates without a local support-base could be parachuted in. The Blair political machine made sure all candidates accepted the Blairite philosophy.

New Labour adopted US-style campaigning and brought into the Labour Party individuals, especially from the city and business, who had never shown an interest in the Labour movement before. Blair's program had been put together by leading professional PR experts and a slick campaign team, including Alistair Campbell, former writer for pornographic magazine Forum, as his spin-doctor.

Labour did bring in the long-awaited minimum wage, and restored trade union rights at GCHQ and implemented other reforms but reneged on promises to repeal the anti-trade-union legislation brought in by the Thatcher government.

The disillusionment of many Labour Party supporters came to a peak with Britain's involvement in the invasion of Iraq. Tony Blair ignored a demonstration of over two million people, many of whom were Labour Party supporters.

But there were no alternatives when it came to parliamentary elections, and so Labour was returned for a second term in 2001. They went on to win a third term in May 2005, albeit with a reduced majority for Blair. Labour politicians boasted that Britain was the fourth largest economy in the world, ignoring the fact that disposable income had decreased and the promise to eradicate child poverty became only 'an aspiration'. Britain became a divided society, the gulf between rich and poor greater than at any time since the Second World War.

Tony Blair took a more realistic view on the Ulster problem (from the time of Michael Foot's leadership the party had had unofficial links with the Republican movement) and, working with the US administration, Labour managed to get the warring parties to reach a compromise. Much of the painstaking work was done by the Northern Ireland Secretary Mo Mowlam, who commented wryly when she got a bigger ovation at the Labour Party conference than Tony Blair, "well that's my parliamentary career over."

Part of the Blair/Brown economic strategy was to raise the gross national product by drastically increasing the population. This was done by encouraging citizens of the EU countries to migrate to Britain. And the population did rise – at the fastest rate ever experienced in the British nation state. Unfortunately there was no formal planning in terms of schools, housing, education places or social and health service provision to meet the rise in the population.

The introduction of the minimum wage helped relieve some of the fall in wages, but the rise in house prices and rents outstripped people's incomes.

There was disquiet on the left when the bank of England was de-nationalised, as its nationalisation had been a cornerstone of the 1945 economic program under the Attlee government, on the recommendation of Maynard Keynes.

.In his first six years in office Blair ordered British troops into battle more often than any other prime minister in British history, including actions in Iraq, Kosovo, Sierra Leone and Afghanistan. Blair, along with Alistair Campbell, produced what is now referred to as the 'dodgy dossier', in which he claimed that Saddam Hussein had weapons of mass destruction that could reach British territory in 45 minutes. No weapons were ever found. For the Iraqi people, the war was a disaster. After untold numbers of deaths, there were no plans for reconstruction, the country descended into civil war and a vicious Islamic fighting

78

force emerged that founded an Islamic State in northern Iraq. Its atrocities spread to America, Africa and Western Europe.

Blair made no secret that he thought distancing New Labour from the trade unions was essential to carry out what he described as Labour's modernisation. Blair instigated the Warwick agreement whereby the trade unions could discuss their problems to see if there was a way to form a mutual agreement. Unfortunately it took some trade union leaders a long time to understand this was just a mechanism to obtain money from the trade unions while they were negotiating with the city and rich donors. Changes were instigated which gave the unions less power at conference. Blair also changed party policy in relation to supporting the closed shop concept and repealing anti-trade union laws which were introduced by Margaret Thatcher.

Blair makes it abundantly clear in his autobiography where his political allegiance lies - he is without doubt the most right-wing leader ever of the Labour Party, an example of this being he believes that the ending of grammar schools was academic vandalism.

Gordon Brown became the new Labour Prime Minister in 2007; however, the lessons of Iraq had not been learned. Britain increased its military role in Afghanistan. Alistair Darling presided over the economy, and the warning signs were there in 2008 over the collapse of Northern Rock – but there were no major changes in financial policy. Then 2009 saw the collapse of Freemanite monetarism, leading to recession. The New Labour government returned to Keynesian economics, part nationalising the collapsed banking system as unemployment reached three million. Then, amid a major scandal over MPs' expenses, the speaker was forced to resign.

There was nothing but panic when Lehman Bros collapsed, leading to a worldwide financial crisis, which of course the working class and the marginalised had to pay for. The total amount of money the people had to pay for the bailout was a staggering £850billion, equal to 33% of GDP - the cost of the NHS per annum at this time was only £111billion. Darling stated it was the worst financial crisis since the Second World War, which in fact given the economic circumstances around the Labour '45 government it certainly wasn't, and, instead of learning the lessons of the Attlee government Darling and Brown opted for austerity.

Much of the energy that should have been given to the running of the economy was spent on a feud with Tony Blair which divided the Cabinet. Brown dithered about going to the electorate and waited until 2010 – Labour disastrously losing 91 seats in the House of Commons.

David Cameron, leader of the Conservatives went into coalition with the smaller Liberal Party who immediately abandoned all of their election manifesto promises, especially those involving student fees.

After the general election defeat in May 2010, Gordon Brown resigned. David Miliband, a staunch Blair supporter, was thought to be the favourite, however on the second ballot his brother Ed Miliband received 50.65% of the total vote.

Ed Miliband then tried to manoeuvre the Labour Party into a middle-of-the-road economic policy - neither full monetarism nor pure Keynes. However the Blairite supporters of neo-liberalism still fought for austerity, whilst the left argued for a reflation of the economy, rejecting austerity outright. Ed Balls, who was Miliband's chancellor, was firmly in the neo-liberal economic camp.

Under Miliband's leadership there was further reform inside the party. Although the membership was still falling, public opinion seemed to be shifting back towards Labour. But it appeared to many that Milibands political philosophy was neither fish nor fowl - he hadn't attacked austerity with a socialist program but accepted softer cuts over a longer period which did not excite the electorate.

On 7 May 2015 the Tories under David Cameron had won an overall majority, with Labour losing 27 seats. Miliband announced his intention to resign as party leader.

A New Kind of Politics

Jeremy Corbyn was first elected to Parliament in 1983. Before that, he had been a full-time union official in NUPE. From his earliest days Corbyn campaigned for left-wing causes. He was also an active member of the CND movement. In the House of Commons, he was vociferous in his attacks against privilege and discrimination, firmly on the left of the Parliamentary Labour Party. After consultation with the socialist group in the PLP, Corbyn announced his intention to stand as leader after Labour's defeat in the 2015 general election and the resultant resignation of Ed Miliband.

Such was the disillusionment on the left at the time that even his most fervent supporters thought his chances of winning were very slim indeed. However, the voting for the leadership of the Labour Party was now more democratic, giving rank-and-file members more power.

The right of the party believed that this would enhance their own chances. Some were so convinced of this they supported Corbyn's nomination because they felt "the left should have a voice." This, they thought, would prove once and for all that the left had no real support amongst rank-and-file members. They dismissed the early poll returns, still convinced he had no chance of winning, especially when the televised hustings took place.

To their amazement, when the much-publicised hustings began, the telephones at Labour HQ were inundated, as was the website, with people who wished to re-join the Labour Party, as well as people who had never been in a political party before but approved of Jeremy Corbyn's left-wing policies, especially his anti-war stance and his anti-austerity statements. This was the first clue people in the PLP picked up that slick PR did not work on many people.

The press rushed to attack and ridicule Corbyn even at this early stage. However, the more they did this the more his support grew, especially amongst the young. When the results were announced, even Corbyn supporters were astonished. On 12 September 2015, Corbyn comfortably won with 59.5% of first-preference votes in all sections. Following his victory, party membership soared.

The Blairite section of the Party couldn't come to terms with either Corbyn' s victory or his rejection of top-down politics, which had been a hallmark of the Blair administration. Corbyn saw the grassroots and party conference as the guiding arm where policy-making was concerned. This was an anathema to Blairites. They were accustomed to policy being handed down from above, and candidates for parliamentary seats being chosen by political advisers and researchers. There were very few traditional working-class men and women obtaining parliamentary seats.

Despite successes in council by-elections and the rise in Corbyn's popularity in the opinion polls, the right of the party constantly attacked Corbyn and there was a great bias not only in the written press but the entire corporate media, including the BBC, which was something of a contradiction in the eyes of political commentators outside the BBC. It was increasingly clear the Conservative government wished to radically change the BBC but traditionally it was the left of the Labour Party that wished to keep the status quo. Now, no-one was happy with corporate media reporting. The same could be said, to a great extent, of Channel 4 News, which increasingly became the voice of the urban elite.

From the very first it became clear that the right in the PLP would not accept the mandate given to Jeremy Corbyn and tried to stage a coup - the majority supporting a motion of no confidence in Jeremy Corbyn. There were arguments whether Corbyn should be automatically on the ballot paper, this was settled by the NEC (although Unite the Union played a leading role) who ruled that he should be. This time Corbyn's opposition was Owen Smith, but he secured an even bigger victory than the first with 61.8%, up from 59.5% of the vote.

The membership went over the half million mark making it the biggest party in Western Europe, however this did not stop the Blairites who along with yesterday's men such as Baron Kinnock, Mandelson, and Blair himself, continued to attack Corbyn.

At the time of writing, they still take every opportunity to undermine Corbyn, his team and his policies. This, in terms of the Labour Party, is history repeating itself. It remains to be seen whether the clearly expressed view of the party membership (the majority enthusiastically pro-Corbyn) will prevail.

The European Union membership referendum took place on 23rd June 2016. 51.9% of voters voting out, on a turnout of 72%. A majority in England and Wales voted to leave while Scotland, Northern Ireland and Gibraltar voted to stay in. Many areas that had been traditionally Labour, especially the industrial working class, felt abandoned by the policies of new Labour.

After the leave vote, David Cameron immediately resigned as leader of the Conservatives, and was replaced as Prime Minister by his home secretary, Theresa May, without a party vote.

Election

After constantly affirming that the fixed-term parliament would be adhered to, and that she would do the full-term, Prime Minister Theresa May called a snap-general election on 8 June 2017. This was done for purely internal party reasons: there was consternation in the Tory ranks when Chancellor Philip Hammond announced in his budget, in contradiction of the party manifesto, that there would be tax increases. May's government had adopted a harsher neo-liberal economic strategy, whereby there would be cuts in corporation tax and no increase in taxation for the very rich; these strategies inevitably lead to cuts in public expenditure. May also wished to have a bigger parliamentary majority to drive through her Brexit strategy.

The national opinion polls at first gave May a substantial lead, but as the campaign continued Jeremy Corbyn came into his own and gained public support, especially when the manifesto 'for the many, not the few' was launched; this was a return to Attlee-type socialism, where the Trade Unions played an important role in the formation of the manifesto.

The detractors stated that this would be the final nail in the coffin of the Corbyn experiment, but as the campaign went on and thousands flocked to hear Corbyn it was clear the manifesto was exactly what a large section of the population wanted.

Theresa May launched a presidential-style campaign with the slogan 'strong and stable' and wanted to concentrate on Brexit, but her ill-conceived manifesto ensured this would not be the case, as it proposed cuts to every section of society. May then back-tracked, doing a U-turn on many of the cuts proposed, while at the same time denying there were any changes, making her look unstable and unsure. Still, the opinion polls, apart from one, had the Conservatives in a commanding lead. However, on election night Labour gained 30 seats, while the Conservatives lost 13, with a turnout being a post-war record with a 9.5 swing to Labour. There was humble-pie from the members of the PLP who tried to deselect Corbyn and had undermined his leadership, which was now stronger than ever. In desperation, the Conservatives turned to the Democratic Unionist Party to give them a majority in parliament. Deeply conservative in their social outlook, the DUP were opposed to gay marriage, wanted to bring back capital punishment, and were opposed to abortion and many of the rights gained by women. Everyone agreed it wouldn't be too long before there was another election. Leading Conservatives publicly stated they had to back May, as another election would certainly bring about the Corbyn government.

Part II   Quick Look-ups

Leaders of the Labour Party

	In Office From:	In Office To:
Keir Hardie	17 February 1906	22 January 1908
Arthur Henderson	22 January 1908	14 February 1910
George Nicoll Barnes	14 February 1910	6 February 1911
Ramsay MacDonald	6 February 1911	5 August 1914
Arthur Henderson	5 August 1914	24 October 1917
William Adamson	24 October 1917	14 February 1921
J. R. Clynes	14 February 1921	21 November 1922
Ramsay MacDonald	21 November 1922	28 August 1931
Arthur Henderson	28 August 1931	25 October 1932
George Lansbury	25 October 1932	8 October 1935
Clement Attlee	8 October 1935	14 December 1955
Hugh Gaitskell	14 December 1955	18 January 1963 Died in office
George Brown	18 January 1963	14 February 1963

Harold Wilson	14 February 1963	5 April 1976
James Callaghan	5 April 1976	10 November 1980
Michael Foot	10 November 1980	2 October 1983
Neil Kinnock	2 October 1983	18 July 1992
John Smith	18 July 1992	12 May 1994 Died in office
Margaret Beckett	May 1994	21 July 1994
Tony Blair	21 July 1994	24 June 2007
Gordon Brown	24 June 2007	11 May 2010
Harriet Harman (Acting)	11 May 2010	25 September 2010
Ed Miliband	25 September 2010	8 May 2015
Harriet Harman (Acting)	8 May 2015	12 September 2015
Jeremy Corbyn	12 September 2015	

Socialist Beginnings and Organisations

Social Democratic Federation

1881 saw the foundation of the Social Democratic Federation, a small Marxist party with its own paper, Justice. The SDF was founded by Henry Mayers Hyndman, a banker and former Conservative. Early members of the SDF included William Morris, George Lansbury and Eleanor Marx. Frederick Engels, however, dismissed Hyndman's brand of Marxism, describing it as "a mixture of Marxism and imperialism" and termed it 'Anglo Marxism.' It was disbanded in 1920. Some members joined the newly formed Communist Party.

In 1884, William Morris founded the Socialist League with other defectors from the SDF, describing the organisation's policies as Revolutionary International Socialism. Morris described himself as a Marxist but with very much an Anglo Marxist interpretation. The organisation had no real base within the trade union movement.

Independent Labour Party

The Independent Labour Party was founded in 1893. Overtly socialist members included Tom Mann, Tom McCarthy, Keir Hardie, George Lansbury and Clement Attlee. In the 1892 General Election, held in July, three working men were elected as independent socialists - Keir Hardie in South West Ham, John Burns in Battersea, and Havelock Wilson in Middlesbrough. The doctrine was not revolution but socialism through Parliament. One of their their main platforms was universal suffrage. They had strong links and support from the trade unions and were founding members of the Labour Representation Committee.

The Fabian Society

The Fabian Society was founded at the London School of Economics in January 1884, with a philosophy of reformist socialism. Its founding members were Edward Carpenter, John Davidson, Havelock Ellis and Edward Pearce, who were founding members of the LRC. Their major contribution to the Labour movement came through Sydney and Beatrice Webb. The early Fabians were in favour of a capitalist welfare state, and supported the New Labour programme. One of their main strategies was to denationalise the bank of England. They were in favour of changes in the Labour Party constitution, including the exclusion of Clause IV, which was ironic as Fabian members Sidney Webb and Arthur Henderson Fabian were the architects of Clause IV.

The Labour Representation Committee

The LRC was formed in 1900 to promote a distinct Labour group in parliament to represent affiliated trade unions, socialist societies and working class opinion in the House of Commons.

The Co-operative Societies were invited to the founding conference, along with the Marxist Social Democratic Federation, the Independent Labour Party, and the Fabian Society, with only the Co-operative Union rejecting the invitation.

The minutes of the foundation report of the LRC show clearly that this was not an organisation with socialism as its main goal. That is not to say there was not a socialist presence at the first conference. Of the 129 delegates, four were from the Marxist Social Democratic Federation and seven from the Independent Labour Party, and there were individual trade union delegates, particularly from the railway workers' unions.

The success of socialists in arguing their cause led to the decline of the LRC. Membership was at an all-time high in 1904 with membership at 969,000, with 165 unions and 76 trades councils affiliated. This fell to 900,000 members the following year, with 158 trade unions and 73 trades councils affiliated. There was still a strong argument, especially from the skilled unions, to stay with either the Liberals or a Lib-Lab pact. Some in the movement were still not in favour of a totally independent Labour Party in Parliament.

The rise of the New Union Movement of the late 1880's had, for a short time, changed the politics of the TUC from reformist to embryonic socialist in its outlook, in its policy for industrial action and its relationship with the state (especially the Liberal Party) and, for the first time, socialism had a national platform. Unfortunately, by 1900, the reformist old guard of the TUC had regained the ascendancy.

The LRC did, however, call for the franchise to be extended to all working men (a third of working men still did not have the vote, and women had no votes at all). The Taff Vale judgement of 1901, by which the establishment tried to wreck the trade union movement, had acted as a great stimulus in bringing the unions together to defend themselves.

It is somewhat ironic that one of the main driving forces behind the LRC was the railway workers, who (as the RMT) were eventually expelled from the party by Tony Blair.

It should be remembered that there were socialist parties, and indeed Marxist ones, that stood candidates for Parliament before the LRC was formed. On the trade union front only Tom Mann, James Connolly, and Jim Larkin stayed loyal to the socialist principles of the New Union Movement which was very much alive in the shop stewards movement, under the banner of syndicalism.

Their actions were viewed much in the same way by employers and by the right of the Labour Movement. The disenfranchised had their voice heard in unofficial industrial action especially amongst women factory and manual workers.

The Communist Party of Great Britain

The CPGB was founded in July 1920. It was made up of an affiliation of Marxists and socialist parties, including the British Socialist Party (BSP) which was far and away the largest party affiliating.

The BSP had been a founding member of the LRC and, given the acceptance of Clause IV, the CPGB sought to affiliate to the Labour Party, but was rebuffed. In 1922, J T W Newbold (Motherwell) was elected to Parliament, as was S Saklatvaia (North Battersea), but as a Labour MP, although he was a member of the Communist Party. After defeat in 1923, he was again elected in 1924, this time as a Communist. Since 1924 the Labour Party has ruled that no member of the Communist Party could be an individual member of the Labour Party, and in 1935, 1943 and 1946, the Labour Party turned down further Communist requests for affiliation. In 1935 and again in 1945, W Gallaher was elected as a Communist for West Fife, and in 1945 Phil Piratin was elected for the Mile End division of Stepney.

There was a major split in the Communist Party in the 1970's between the communists who rejected Leninism and those that still accepted Marxist-Leninist philosophy. The latter, after industrial action, managed to keep control of the Morning Star, at that time Britain's only daily socialist paper. The membership of the Communist Party is now around 1000 members. Their influence in the trade unions is still strong.

The Morning Star is the only socialist daily newspaper published in Great Britain its first title was the Daily Worker it was founded at the beginning of 1930 as a voice of the Communist Party becoming the morning star in 1966. The paper is owned by its readership.

The Commonwealth Party

Founded in 1942 during the wartime electoral truce between Labour and the Conservatives, its philosophy was to contest all by-elections where reactionary candidates were contesting seats and where not opposed by a Labour or other progressive candidate. Three by-elections were won in this way. In 1943, membership of the Commonwealth Party was proscribed by the Labour Party. In 1945, Commonwealth members of Parliament joined the ranks of Labour.

The National Labour Party

Formed in 1931 from the group of Labour MPs who supported the national government under Ramsay MacDonald, in the 1931 election, 13 of its 20 candidates were elected. In 1935, eight of its 20 candidates were elected. The party wound itself up in 1940.

Labour Party Constitution and Clause IV

'To secure for the workers by hand or by brain the full fruits of their industry and the most equitable distribution thereof that may be possible upon the basis of the common ownership of the means of production, distribution, and exchange, and the best obtainable system of popular administration and control of each industry or service.'

In 1918 Arthur Henderson, along with Sidney Webb, reorganised the Labour Party. Their main aims were to provide local Labour Parties in every constituency or group of constituencies.

These local Labour Parties were to be based fundamentally on individual subscribing membership, though representation was provided for trades councils, trade union branches, and socialist societies. The members of the National Executive Committee (NEC) were to be elected by the annual conference as a whole (though eleven were to be elected from candidates nominated by the trade unions and socialist societies as a single group, five were to represent the local Labour Parties, and four were to be women). The scheme also involved an increase in affiliation fees.

Henderson and Webb were confident they could control the party through this method. The constitution was modified in 1937 in favour of the local constituency Labour Parties, which had repeatedly demanded a greater share in the control of party affairs.

Representation of the constituency parties on the NEC was increased from five to seven. The seven were to be elected by the vote of the constituency delegates alone. The twelve trade union representatives and one representative of the socialist societies were to be elected separately by their respective conference delegations.

The five women members were to be nominated by any affiliated organisation and elected by a vote of the whole party conference. The Leader (since 1929) and the Deputy Leader (since 1953) were ex-officio members of the NEC. The Treasurer of the Party was to be nominated by any affiliated organisation, and elected by the vote of the whole party conference.

The original plan was amended, so that the NEC was increased to a membership of 23 (adding two to the number specified for affiliated organisations). This was the high point in terms of democracy within the Labour party. The right in the Labour Party made several attempts to reverse the power of the rank-and-file on the NEC, EC and at conference, and several attempts to remove Clause IV from the constitution. In the late 1940's, Herbert Morrison tried unsuccessfully to change the constitution in favour of the Parliamentary Labour Party. Both Hugh Gaitskell and James Callaghan were also unsuccessful in their bids to radically change the constitution and abandon Clause IV. It was left to Herbert Morrison's grandson (Peter Mandelson) to successfully resurrect the changes called for by the right, taking away power from the membership affiliates and constituencies and abandoning Clause IV.

Abridged history of industrial relations law

Pre-1945

Prior to the Black Death and the Peasants Revolt of 1381, agricultural labour had been contained under feudalism.

The first recognisable labour legislation was the **Ordinance of Labourers 1349**, following the Black Death. It was concerned with maintaining wages at rates to be fixed by Justices of the Peace. The aim was to control the level of wages, to outlaw any combination of Labour, and to discuss terms and conditions of employment. The Act was further enforced by the **1562 Act**.

The state recognised the danger of combination following the embryonic Industrialization of the United Kingdom and the French and American Revolutions. In 1797 the state passed the **Unlawful Oaths Act** and in 1799 the **Unlawful Societies Act**. These were obvious devices to stop trade unions being formed. It was these laws the Tolpuddle martyrs were prosecuted under. They were sentenced to transportation to Australia.

The **Combination Acts 1799** made it a criminal act to combine to raise wages for better conditions, to incite others to join a combination of trade unionists, to persuade a co-worker or any worker to insist on better wages or conditions, or to incite that person to leave his present occupation to find better terms and conditions. Justices could order up to three months imprisonment for this.

But this did not stop the rise of trade unionism. After much lobbying and a demonstration, elements of the combination act were repealed in 1824 – but the state introduced the **Master and Servant Act 1823** which stated that an employee absent from service before his/her contract expired was punishable by up to three months hard labour. There were some 10,000 prosecutions between the years 1858 and 1875.

Despite all the efforts of the state, the trade union and Labour movement gained influence and power. The TUC was formed in 1868, and by the 1870's the state had been pushed to repeal much of the most draconian legislation. The **Criminal Amendment Act 1871** liberalised much of the former legislation – but much remained, and the employers turned more and more to the civil court with ever increasing use of injunctions, especially in relation to breach of contract.

In 1898 the House of Lords rejected any extension to the act, then in 1900 they reversed their decision. In 1901 the House of Lords tried to deal a body blow to the Labour Movement in the **Taff Vale railway case**, where the employers took the Amalgamated Society of railway Servants to Court, suing them for loss of profit. The union had to pay £42,000 compensation, including costs.

After much lobbying the Liberal government passed the **Trades Disputes Act 1906** which excluded the union and union members from liability.

In 1910 the Amalgamated Society of Railway Servants were in court once more. The **Osborne judgment** stated that trade unions could not spend money on political purposes. This Act was repealed in 1913. In 1919 the Whitley councils were founded. There was no trade union legislation until after the failure of the General Strike in 1926. The **Trades Dispute Act 1927** made political strikes illegal – the court decided what was political. During the Second World War, 1939-45, strikes were made illegal.

1945 onward

The 1945 Labour Government repealed all anti-trade union legislation in 1946. It also endorsed the Pre-closed shop and gave full trade union recognition. There was no further major trades union legislation until the '60's.

The **Trades Disputes Act 1965** clarified some irregularities constituted by a law lords ruling, Rooks v Barnard 1964, which would have made all past disputes illegal.

The 1970's saw major anti-trade-union legislation. The new conservative government moved swiftly with the -**Industrial Relations Act 1971**. The main Points of the Act were:

- Ending pre-entry closed shop

- The right of member not to take industrial action and even if a ballot is taken

- Establishing the National Industrial Relations Court

- Making collective bargaining for the first time legally enforceable

- Removing immunity from prosecution for secondary and sympathetic strikes

- Making it unlawful for anyone but a full time official to call a strike or any other industrial action

When Labour came to power in 1974, it passed the **Trade Union and Labour Relations Act 1974** and the **Employment Protection Act 1975**. The measures were:

- Guaranteed payments for lay-off and short time, and enforced payment during medical suspension from work

- Strengthened provisions for extension of collectively agreed or general level terms and conditions

- The right to maternity pay and the right to return after maternity

- Protection of wages and other payments on the insolvency of the employer

- A new statutory procedure for recognition of trade unions after the intervention of ACAS, going much further than the Industrial Relations Act provisions which were only open to registered organisations

- Compelling employers to provide information for collective bargaining purposes to recognised unions

- Recognising unions' right to be consulted about redundancies.

- Shop stewards' and trade union members' right to time off for union duties and activities respectively

- Strengthening the right to a written statement of contractual terms, and added a regular itemed pay statement

The **Equal Pay Act**, actually passed in 1970, was bought into force in 1975 along with the **Sex Discrimination Act**, and the **Race Relations Act 1976**.

The new Conservative government quickly brought in the - **Employment Act 1980**. The main points were:

- Public money for trade union secret ballots

- Limiting the effectiveness of the closed shop

- Limiting the rights of workers for unfair dismissal

- Limiting women's maternity rights

- Making illegal secondary action

- Limiting picketing

- Abolishing statutory recognition of trade unions

More anti-trade union legislation was brought to the statute books in the **Employment Act 1982**. The measures were:

- Removing immunity from trade union funds.

- Subjecting closed shops to review

- Prohibiting union membership-only causes in contracts and tender document

- Increasing compensation for employees unfairly dismissed in consequence of a closed shop

Further anti-trade union legislation was stopped by **European directives**, which intervened on such matters as protection of employers' rights and equal pay. The European reforms were introduced with the government minister Alan Clark stating that he did so "without any enthusiasm". But in 1986 the **Truck Acts** were abolished along with wage council protection and redundancy rebates were removed.

The **Employment Act 1988** included:

- Giving further rights to trade union members opposed to any industrial or strike action by means of ballots

- Tightening the rules in relation to the unions' political funds

- Tightening the provisions on the closed shop

The **Employment Act 1989** added the following:

- The abolition of the National Dock Labour Scheme and the protection of registered dock workers

- Amendments to the Sex Discrimination Act

- Restriction of the right of trade union officials to have time off for trade union duties

- Removal of the rights of redundancy rebates even for small businesses

The **Employment Act 1990** included the following measures:

- The abolition of pre-entry closed shop

- Further restrictions on secondary action

- Weakening the powers of the Commissioner for trade union members rights

- Making trade unions liable for the actions of officers and shop stewards

- Preventing members claiming unfair dismissal if dismissed while on unofficial action

The Major Government implemented the **Trade Union Reform and Employment Rights Act 1993**

- Placing further restrictions on the rights of employees to strike

- Strictly regulating the financial affairs of trade unions

European Directives 1993:

- Made provisions to extend workers' rights in particular maternity rights

- Reform of employment tribunal procedure

- The Human Rights Act 1993

- Working hours directive `

The 1994 Major Government abolished minimum hours thresholds.

European Directives 1995:

- Conciliation had to take place over redundancies and transfer of understanding whether or not the union is recognized

- A new consolidation measure, the **Employment Rights Act 1996**, brought together the Provision of the Employment Protection

- **(Consolidation) Act 1979**, the **Wages Act 1986**, the **Employment Acts 1980 and 1982**, and parts of several other statutes

- **Disability discrimination Act 1995**

New Labour Legislation 1997-2004

- **National Minimum Wage Act 1998**

- New statutory procedures for the recognition and the regulation of Trade Unions for collective bargaining

- Provisions relating to protection for trade union membership and non-trade union membership

- New rights and changes in family-related employment rights

- A new right for workers to be accompanied in disciplinary and grievance hearings

- Other changes in individual employment rights

European Directives 2002

- Family rights

- Paid paternity leave

- Reform to aspects of employment tribunals

- Fixed term contracts

- Flexible working

- Maternity leave

- Part time workers' rights to pay and holiday

2004-8 legislation: the changes made were minimal and the New Labour government made it abundantly clear that they would not repeal the anti-trade union legislation brought in by Thatcher, nor would they accept any elements in the **European Social Chapter** to give workers extra rights

Measures to tackle the intimidation of workers during recognition and derecognition ballots by introducing rules which define improper campaigning activity by employers and unions.

Following discussions between unions and labour ministers, the **"Warwick Agreement (trade unions and labour)" 2004** set out agreed policy proposals including:

- An end to the two-tier workforce across the entire public sector

- 8 public holidays plus four weeks annual leave – but with an opt-out

- Family Friendly policies- improved time off to attend to a sick relative

- Flexible working for workers caring for a disabled family member

- Gangmaster regulation and an end to exploitation of migrant workers

- Will support an EU Directive on Agency Workers next electoral term

- Will introduce legislation this term on Corporate manslaughter

- Steps to close the equality gap

- The introduction of sectoral bargaining in trial sectors

This fell short of trade union demands for repeal of anti-trade union (Tory) laws.

2015 proposed **Trade Unions Act** the Conservative government introduced draconian anti-trade union legislation which is comparable to the 1927 anti trade union act following the general strike. The measures to stop trade unions financing the Labour Party are on a par with the Osborne judgement of 1909.

Trade Union Act 2017

The Act reforms the rules on trade union ballots for taking industrial action. The main provisions of the Act are:

- 50% turnout threshold for there to be a valid ballot on industrial action

- Threshold of 40% support from all members in order to take industrial action in key sectors

- Four month time limit for which the ballot will remain valid to authorise industrial action

The Course of Events

1688	Glorious revolution (bourgeois)
1694	Formation of the bank of England
1776	American declaration of independence
1789	French revolution begins
1791	Paine's rights of man published
1792	London corresponding society formed
1795	"Speenhamland" scale of relief adopted
1799	First Combination Act; suppression of corresponding societies
1800	Combination Act
1801	General Enclosure Act
1811	Luddite riots
1819	Peterloo Massacre
1824	Combination acts repealed
1825	Combination law made less liberal

1829	Owenite Co-operative Societies founded
1830	Agricultural labourers' riots
1832	Reform Act
1833	First Factory Act
1834	Grand national consolidated trades union
1834	New poor law Trial of Dorchester Labourers (Tolpuddle Martyrs)
1838	People's Charter issued
1839	Chartist convention and petition Newport rising
1842	Second Chartist petition General strike.
1844	Rochdale pioneers start Co-operative store
1845	National Association of United Trades formed
1846	Combination Laws repealed
1847	Ten Hours Act
1848	Third Chartist petition

1851	Amalgamated Society of Engineers formed
1860	London Trades Council formed
1861	Amalgamated Society of Carpenters and Joiners formed
1863	Co-operative Wholesale Society formed
1864	First Trades Union Congress
1867	Reform Act
1870	Education Act
1871	Formation of the Stevedores and Dockers Union Trade Union Act Criminal Law Amendment Act
1872	National Agricultural Labourers Union formed Trade Union Amendment Act Major changes in company law
1881	Social Democratic Federation formed
1883	Fabians Society Formed
1884	Reform Act
1888	New Union Movement

	Miners Federation formed
	Match girls strike
	Gasworks strike
1889	Formation of unskilled workers into unions resulting in major labour unrest including the London docks strike
	Scottish Labour Party formed
1892/3	Independent Labour MPs elected
1893	Independent Labour Party formed
1900	Labour Representation Committee formed
1901	Taff Vale judgment
1906	Labour Representation Committee becomes the Parliamentary Labour Party
1908	Plebs league – a movement for independent working-class education
1909	Osborne judgement
1911	Transport strikes
1912	Miners strike
	Daily Herald first published

1913	National Union of Railwaymen formed
1914	World War I begins
1915	Clyde strikes Shop Stewards Movement
1917	Russian revolution
1918	World War I ends
1919	Versailles treaty Boom begins League of Nations founded
1920	Communist Party founded
1921	Boom ends Miners lockout Black Friday
1922	Engineering lockout Fascist coup in Italy
1924	First Labour government
1926	General strike

1927	Trades Disputes Act
1929	Second Labour government
1930	Daily Worker first published
1931	"National" government formed
1932	Japan invades Manchuria
1933	Nazi Party comes to power in Germany
1935	Abyssinian crisis Mass unemployment in UK Government rejects Keynesian economics Roosevelt brings in the Keynesian New Deal in the USA
1937	Japan invades China
1938	Nazis invade Austria Munich settlement.
1939	Nazis invade Czechoslovakia Nazi-Soviet pact World War II begins
1940	Chamberlain's government overturned

	Fall of France to Nazis
1941	Nazis invade Russia Japan attacks USA at Pearl Harbour
1945	Victory over Germany and Japan Labour government elected and begins National Health Service, education reform, trade union reform and nationalisation of all major industries
1951	Labour government defeated Conservative government elected but accepts labour reforms, adopts one-nation policy
1964	Labour government elected Major social reforms
1970	Conservative government elected
1974	Labour government elected
1979	Conservative government elected, Margaret Thatcher becomes leader, rejects one-nation Toryism and Keynesian economics in favour of monetarism Confrontation with the trade union movement
1990	Collapse of the Soviet Union
1994	New Labour drops Clause IV

1997	Tony Blair elected Prime Minister Continues monetarism policy, although Labour bring in the minimum wage, restore trade-union rights at GCHQ, and implement other reforms
2001	Labour is returned for second term
2003	Despite Iraq War demonstration, Blair joins Bush in the invasion of Iraq
2005	The Labour Party win a third term for Blair with a reduced majority
2007	Gordon Brown becomes New Labour Prime Minister
2008	Britain intensifies its military role in Afghanistan
2009	Banking crisis: government bails out banks to the tune of billions New Labour Government returns to Keynesian economics, and part nationalises the collapsed banking system. Unemployment reaches 3 million.
2010	Equality Act passed Coalition Conservstive-Liberal government formed. The Liberals abandon Keynes and accept neo-liberal policy Ed Miliband is elected Leader of the Labour Party
2011	Marches against austerity measures

	Public Sector Strikes
2013	Government plans to re-draw constituency boundaries but is defeated
2014	Affordable Homes Bill, designed to relax controversial housing benefit cuts Scotland votes "No" to Scottish Independence by a margin of 55.3% to 44.7% MPs
2015	General election resulting in the Conservative Party winning an outright majority Scottish National Party achieves huge gains Liberal Democrats are almost wiped out Jeremy Corbyn is elected leader of the Labour Party
2016	United Kingdom votes to leave the European union 51.89% vote to leave while 48.1% vote to remain David Cameron resigns as leader of the Conservative party to be replaced by Theresa May Austerity continues Jeremy Corbyn stands again as leader of the Labour Party against Owen Smith. Corbyn secures 61.8% of the vote to Smith's 38.2%. The victory strengthens his hold on a party that has expanded dramatically since the 2015 general election and now has more than 500,000 members

2017	Len McCluskey socialist general secretary of unite the trade union re-elected
2017	Snap election called by Theresa May. Against all predictions the Tories lose 13 seats while Labour gain 30. The Tories lose their majority, and May signs a pact with the DUP to keep her in office

Lightning Source UK Ltd.
Milton Keynes UK
UKHW020937120920
369736UK00005B/350

9 780955 692345